Deathly Delights

Deathly Delights

Dark Tourism's Thrills and Chills

Rafeal Mechlore

WSM Publisher

CONTENTS

INDEX 1

INTRODUCTION 3

Chapter 1 16

Chapter 2 33

Chapter 3 47

Chapter 4 62

Chapter 5 80

Chapter 6 97

Chapter 7 112

Chapter 8 124

Chapter 9 138

INDEX

Introduction

1. Definition of Dark Tourism
2. The growing popularity of dark tourism
3. The allure of morbid attractions
4. Purpose and scope of the book

Chapter 1: The Fascination with the Macabre
1.1 Exploring the human fascination with death
1.2 Historical perspectives on morbid curiosity
1.3 Psychological aspects of dark tourism
1.4 Contemporary drivers of interest in the macabre

Chapter 2: Dark Tourism Through the Ages
2.1 Historical roots of dark tourism
2.2 Early examples of morbid attractions
2.3 Transformation and evolution over time

Chapter 3: Modern Morbid Attractions
3.1 Key dark tourism destinations around the world
3.2 Famous sites, such as Auschwitz, Chernobyl, and Alcatraz
3.3 Emerging trends and destinations in dark tourism

Chapter 4: The Ethical Dilemmas of Dark Tourism
4.1 Ethical concerns and debates surrounding morbid attractions
4.2 The impact of visitor behavior on sensitive sites
4.3 Balancing education, remembrance, and entertainment

Chapter 5: Commercialization and Controversy

5.1 The commodification of dark tourism
5.2 Marketing and branding of morbid attractions
5.3 Controversies surrounding commercialized death

Chapter 6: The Thrills and Chills of Dark Tourism
6.1 Experiences and emotions of dark tourists
6.2 How dark tourism fulfills a unique niche in travel
6.3 The fine line between fascination and discomfort

Chapter 7: Dark Tourism and Pop Culture
7.1 The representation of dark tourism in literature, film, and television
7.2 How popular culture influences our perception of morbid attractions

Chapter 8: Behind-the-Scenes of Dark Tourism
8.1 Interviews with tour guides and operators
8.2 Insights into the management and curation of dark tourist sites
8.3 The challenges and rewards of working in dark tourism

Chapter 9: The Future of Dark Tourism
9.1 Trends and predictions for the future of morbid attractions
9.2 Sustainability and responsible tourism in dark tourism
9.3 How global events and shifts in society impact the industry

INTRODUCTION

A new trend that explores the depths of our fascination with the macabre, the unsettling, and the enigmatic has arisen in a world where traditional tourism has often given way to a desire for one-of-a-kind and immersive experiences. This trend has emerged in a world where traditional tourism has often given way to the desire for unique and immersive encounters. We would like to take this opportunity to welcome you to "Deadly Delights: Dark Tourism's Thrills and Chills," a voyage into the alluring and, at times, unsettling world of travel and exploration.

The fascination with death, calamity, and the macabre has been around for as long as humanity has, and it is this allure that the author of this book hopes to investigate. You are cordially invited to go on an exciting journey through "Deadly Delights," which follows the psychological connections that connect us to the most sinister parts of reality. We will investigate the complex nature of our fascination with the macabre, from the time when people first became interested in the macabre until the present day, when people's tastes are always changing.

Beyond the annals of history, we will set out on a journey throughout the world to visit haunted and macabre tourist attractions. You will go to well-known locations such as Auschwitz, Chernobyl, and Alcatraz, and while there, you will discover the historical significance of these places as well as the powerful emotional impact they have on tourists. In addition to this, we will shed light on less well-known locations, challenge preconceived notions about the genre, and offer new and interesting perspectives on it.

"Deathly Delights" does not shy away from the ethical difficulties that are associated with dark tourism, which confronts the tension between respectful remembering and the commercialization of tragedy. It opens the door to a more in-depth analysis of these contentious features by analyzing the intricacies of visitor behavior and the effect of mass tourism on sensitive sites.

Join us as we explore into the marketing and branding of morbid attractions, as well as the ethical concerns surrounding the monetization of death, as we continue our investigation into the intersection of commercialization and controversy. This book will ask some very important issues about where the line should be drawn between honoring the past and using it for financial gain, and it will try to answer those questions.

The feelings that are stirred up are the driving force behind dark tourism. The documentary titled "Deadly Delights" dives at the experiences of dark tourists, the spectrum of feelings they go through, and the thin line that they walk between being fascinated and being uncomfortable. You'll get a realistic image of the one-of-a-kind emotional journey that dark tourists go on by listening to personal experiences and testimonials from people who have been on the path.

Although it may have a macabre reputation, dark tourism is actually very entwined with contemporary pop culture. This book examines its portrayal in many forms of media, including literature, cinema, and television, focusing on the ways in which these mediums influence how we think about macabre tourist destinations and the travel industry as a whole.

In addition to this, you will be given access to the undercover world of dark tourism, which will include interviews with tour guides and operators as well as their unique perspectives. They will discuss the experiences, difficulties, and benefits of working in this mysterious business, providing an up-close and personal look at the individuals who are responsible for making dark tourism feasible.

The final chapters of "Deadly Delights" take a look into a crystal ball to examine the future of dark tourism, the tendencies that will shape it, and the potential impact that global events and societal shifts could have on it. In order to protect the industry's credibility and assure its continued existence, the book promotes the use of tourism techniques that are both responsible and environmentally friendly.

The publication "Deadly Delights: Dark Tourism's Thrills and Chills" is more than just a book; rather, it is a portal to some of the world's most mysterious and thought-provoking locations. It encourages you to reconsider what you know about traveling and makes you think about the limits of curiosity, recall, and amusement in a world where the gloomy and the pleasurable frequently coexist with one another. We invite you to come along with us as we set off on a voyage that will, above all else, enlighten, challenge, and fascinate you.

1. **Definition of Dark Tourism**

    A subfield of the travel business that goes by the name "dark tourism" is designated by this word, which has seen increased usage over the past few years. It entails going to locations that are connected with death, misery, tragedy, or things that are macabre. These locations often have a significant role in history or culture as a result of the occurrence of certain events or conditions that took place there. Dark tourism, as its name suggests, leads tourists into the shadows of our society, revealing the fascination of the spooky, the uncomfortable, and the controversial.

    The Development of Untraditional Tourism:

In order to get a complete comprehension of the idea of dark tourism, we need to investigate its historical development. Since the dawn of time, people have been engaging in dark tourism in a variety of forms. Pilgrimages to sacred sites, such as the catacombs of Rome, where Christians sought refuge during times of persecution are some of the first examples of this practice. People were drawn to locations connected with martyrdom and suffering because these excursions had value not only from a historical but also a spiritual perspective.

In the latter half of the 20th century, the concept of "dark tourism" began to acquire hold. Academic conversations regarding the phenomena started to take shape, and scholars started looking for ways to describe and make sense of this new area. Today, the term "dark tourism" refers to travel to a diverse range of locales, some of which include former concentration camps, battlefields, disaster sites, jails, and places connected with serial killers. Other examples are also included.

Reasons for Engaging in Dark Tourism:

Curiosity: Many people who go to dark tourist attractions are driven to do so by an innate interest in macabre and dismal topics. They are interested in investigating the more disturbing facets of human history and psyche.

Some people are interested in visiting these locations because of their historical or cultural value. This may be the case for some people. Dark tourism can offer visitors a glimpse into the past and help them gain a deeper comprehension of the events that took place in a particular location.

Some people see black tourism as a sort of remembering and respect for the past, while others

see it as something else different. They go to the locations where the atrocities took place to pay their respects to the victims and make sure that history is not forgotten.

Education is one of the primary benefits of participating in dark tourism, as it enables visitors to have a better understanding of the complexities of human history as well as the results of certain actions.

For the thrill and the entertainment value, some "dark tourists" seek out unpleasant locations to experience the rush of adrenaline that comes with traveling to unusual locations. The emotion of fear or the experience of discomfort can serve as a motivating force.

These locations have the potential to serve as venues for visitors to engage in acts of thought and contemplation, which will encourage them to think about the human condition, morality, and society.

Influence of popular culture and the media The media, such as novels, movies, and television, frequently portray tourist hotspots as dangerous places to visit. This publicity has the potential to influence and persuade tourists to visit these locations.

Different kinds of places that offer "dark tourism" are as follows:
The term "sites of atrocity" refers to places like concentration camps, memorials to victims of genocide, and other areas associated with numerous murders. The concentration camp Auschwitz in Poland is a notable example.

Disaster Sites: Places that have been affected by natural or man-made disasters, such as the Chernobyl nuclear power plant in Ukraine, are popular destinations for "dark tourists" who are curious about the aftermath of these kinds of tragedies.

Prisons and Asylums: Abandoned or historic prisons and mental asylums can provide a peek into the criminal justice and mental healthcare systems that existed in the past. This is especially true for abandoned prisons.

Historic battlefields, such as Gettysburg, which may be found in the United States, draw visitors who are interested in the study of military history.

Cemeteries & Tombs: Well-known cemeteries such as Père Lachaise in Paris or the catacombs in a number of cities offer visitors one-of-a-kind experiences that are connected to death and memorialization.

There are some visitors who go to areas where infamous murders took place, such the Lizzie Borden Bed & Breakfast in Massachusetts. These tourists are called "murder and crime scene tourists."

Locations connected with Serial Killers Some people, like Ted Bundy or Jeffrey Dahmer, find themselves drawn to the locations connected with serial killers like them.

Museums of Medicine and Science: These types of establishments provide information on the development of medicine through displays on topics such as operations, pathology, and abnormalities in the human anatomy.

Considerations of an Ethical Nature:

Exploitation: The commercialization of dark tourism might raise issues about profiting off tragedy, which may be considered a disrespectful act toward the memories of those who have suffered.

Sensitivity: It is imperative that tourists be sensitive to the idea that the locations they are visiting represent actual historical events, many of which included tremendous amounts of human suffering.

Value in terms of Education versus Entertainment Dark tourism should not simply aim to entertain or sensationalize, but rather to educate and increase comprehension of the subject matter.

Behavior of Visitors: It is absolutely essential for visitors to behave responsibly in order to guarantee that these locations are revered and treated with respect.

The requirement for preservation must be balanced with the need to give access and education at each site; this is known as the "balance of preservation and access."

effect on the Local Community The presence of dark tourism may have an effect on the local community, and it is important that this impact be taken into consideration and controlled appropriately.

The Prospects for the Industry of Dark Tourism:
Both opportunities and challenges are presented to the industry of dark tourism as it continues to develop. The integrity of these locations, as well as its instructional value, must be maintained via the development of this business in a responsible manner. The future of dark tourism will be heavily influenced by factors such as sustainability, ethical concerns, and responsible tourism practices.

Additionally, when the globe faces new challenges and crises, such as the COVID-19 epidemic, the definition and scope of dark tourism may grow to encompass venues connected with modern events and experiences. This is because the world is constantly confronting new challenges and crises.

2. **The growing popularity of dark tourism**

In recent years, there has been a phenomenal increase in the amount of people participating in dark tourism, which was formerly a relatively unnoticed subset of the travel business. This unusual kind of travel, which focuses on visiting locations connected with death, calamity, misery, or the macabre, has captivated the imagination of an increasing number of tourists looking for experiences that are distinctive and thought-provoking. During the course of this investigation, we are going to explore the reasons behind the growing attractiveness of dark tourism and investigate the aspects that are fueling its expansion.

How to Define "Dark Tourism"
It is essential, before digging into the ever-increasing popularity of dark tourism, to first determine what all falls under the umbrella of this phrase. Traveling to locations that have historical or cultural significance due to their associations with death or suffering is an example of dark tourism, which is also known as grief tourism and thanatourism in some circles. These vacation spots frequently include locations that are tied to tragic occurrences, such as war, genocide, natural catastrophes, jails, asylums, cemeteries, or even places linked to prominent persons, such as serial murderers. Even while the idea of dark tourism has been around for quite some time, in recent years it has become more widely recognized as a unique category of vacationing.

Contextualization historique:
It is possible to trace the origins of dark tourism all the way back through history. Pilgrimages to holy sites that had a connection to martyrdom, death, or miracles could be regarded early manifestations of what is now known as "dark tourism." As individuals tried to connect with their ancestors and pay their respects, they frequently paired their spiritual commitment with an interest in historical research during these journeys.

On the other hand, the term "dark tourism" did not become common parlance until the latter half of the 20th century. Academic conversations started looking into the phenomena, and scholars tried to characterize and make sense of the rising interest in going to these macabre attractions. The beginning of the 21st century was marked by an increase in the popularity of dark tourism, which reflects a larger movement in travel preferences toward more experiential, unique, and eccentric encounters.

The Allure of Tourism in the Dark:

Curiosity and intrigue are two of the key forces that drive dark tourism. One of the primary causes of dark tourism is human curiosity regarding macabre and gloomy topics. These sites have a reputation for being shrouded in mystery, and as a result, they attract travelers who are interested in delving into the most sinister sides of human history and psyche.

Significance to History and Culture A great number of haunted tourist destinations may not be denied for their significance to either history or culture. These places can shed light on events that took place in the past, providing a one-of-a-kind opportunity to gain a deeper comprehension of the influence that such events had on society and the world.

Commemoration and introspection: as a kind of commemoration and respect, some people choose to participate in activities associated with dark tourism. They go there to show their respect for the people who lost their lives in the catastrophe and to make sure that their stories are not forgotten.

Education and enlightenment are two benefits that can be gained from participating in dark tourism. These benefits come in the form of an educational experience that illuminates the complexities of human history as well as the results of specific actions. It encourages analytical thinking about problems facing society, questions of morality, and the nature of being human.

Excitement and Sensation: For some people, the attractiveness of dark tourism rests in the fact that it can give them with a sense of both excitement and sensation. The experience of seeing locations that are unsettling and thought-provoking can be powerful and emotionally charged, often triggering fear, discomfort, or even catharsis. This can be a positive or negative experience for the traveler.

Influence of Popular Culture The media, such as literature, movies, and television shows, frequently portray tourist hotspots as dangerous places to visit. The viewing of these depictions has the potential to stimulate the curiosity of travelers and persuade them to visit these locations.

Travelers have a growing desire to have one-of-a-kind experiences as traditional tourism gets more congested and generic, and as a result, more travelers are looking for ways to differentiate their vacations. The practice of dark tourism gives visitors the chance to investigate locations that are distinct from the conventional tourist attractions.

Different kinds of places that offer "dark tourism" are as follows:
The term "sites of atrocity" refers to places like concentration camps, memorials to victims of genocide, and other areas associated with numerous murders. One of the most well-known concentration camps was located in Poland and was named Auschwitz.

Destinations associated to Natural or Man-Made Disasters: Locations associated to natural or man-made disasters, such as Chernobyl in Ukraine, are destinations that draw gloomy tourism interested in studying the aftermath of tragic events.

Jails and Asylums: Abandoned or historic jails and mental asylums provide insights into the judicial and medical systems that were in place in the past, particularly with regard to the treatment of mental illness.

Historic battlefields, such as Gettysburg in the United States, are a popular tourist destination for people who are interested in the study of military history.

Cemeteries & Tombs: Well-known cemeteries such as Père Lachaise in Paris or the catacombs in a number of cities offer visitors one-of-a-kind experiences that are connected to death and memorialization.

There are some visitors who go to areas where infamous murders took place, such the Lizzie Borden Bed & Breakfast in Massachusetts. These tourists are called "murder and crime scene tourists."

Locations Associated with prominent Serial Killers One subcategory of "dark tourism" comprises destinations that are linked to prominent serial killers such as Ted Bundy or Jeffrey Dahmer.

Museums of Medicine and Science: Visits to museums such as the Mutter Museum in Philadelphia can provide interesting insights into the history of medicine. The museum features displays on a variety of medical topics, such as operations, pathology, and anatomical abnormalities.

The Obstacles and Ethical Considerations that Face Us:
Issues About Exploitation The commercialization of dark tourism can raise issues about benefiting off tragedy, which may be seen as disrespectful to the memories of individuals who have endured suffering.

Respect and compassion: Visitors to these places are expected to approach them with respect and compassion, keeping in mind that they represent true historical events that frequently involved extreme human suffering.

Value in terms of Education versus Entertainment Dark tourism should not simply aim to entertain or sensationalize, but rather to educate and increase comprehension of the subject matter.

Behavior of Visitors: It is absolutely essential for visitors to behave responsibly in order to guarantee that these locations are revered and treated with respect.

The requirement for preservation must be balanced with the need to give access and education at each site; this is known as the "balance of preservation and access."

affect on the Local Community The presence of dark tourism can have an affect on the local community, and this impact can be either favorable or harmful. It is really necessary to manage this impact.

The Prospects for the Industry of Dark Tourism:
Both opportunities and challenges are presented to the industry of dark tourism as it continues to develop. The sites' authenticity and instructional value depend critically on development that is both sustainable and responsible if they are to be preserved in their entirety. This necessitates striking a fine balance between allowing access, promoting education and remembrance, but also showing due regard for the delicate nature of the past.

There is a possibility that in the future of dark tourism, there may be an expansion in the types of locations that are visited. It is possible that contemporary events and experiences, like as the COVID-19 epidemic, will become a part of the dark tourism landscape as the globe continues to confront new difficulties and catastrophes. Visits to pandemic-related places, quarantine facilities, or healthcare institutions could be among these activities.

The rise in popularity of dark tourism is an indication that the tourist industry is moving in the direction of trips that are richer in experience and less conventional. Because today's tourists are looking for experiences that are one-of-a-kind, thought-provoking, and emotionally stimulating, "dark tourism" has emerged as a popular option. This kind of travel provides a wide variety of reasons to go, varied locations to see, and ethical questions to ponder, reflecting the intricate interaction that exists between human curiosity, remembering, educational pursuits, and recreational activities.

As the popularity of dark tourism continues to expand, the development of this industry in a responsible manner is becoming more and more important. This is necessary to ensure that these locations continue to provide insights into our collective history and the human condition.

3. **The allure of morbid attractions**

There is a peculiar and ever-increasing fascination with things that are macabre and disturbing, despite the fact that our lives are frequently dominated by the conventional and the commonplace. One aspect of dark tourism that has attracted the interest and imagination of a wide variety of tourists is the draw of macabre attractions. This investigation focuses at the causes behind the allure of morbid attractions, the psychological and emotional components that bring people to these sites, and the broader cultural and historical background that underpins this interest in order to better understand why people are so drawn to these places.

An Explanation of What Morbid Attractions Are:
It is vital, before digging into the fascination of morbid attractions, to establish

what all of these attractions fall under the umbrella phrase of "morbid attractions." The term "morbid attractions" refers to places to visit, experiences to have, or topics that can be explored at those locations, such as death, pain, tragedy, or the macabre. These locations are significant for their role in history or culture as a result of the events or conditions that they represent. The unpleasant and thought-provoking nature of the experiences that morbid attractions typically have to offer is frequently what contributes to their charm.

A Contextualization of History:
The fascination with things that are gruesome and horrific is not a fresh development. The human race has always been fascinated by everything associated with the afterlife and the afterworld. One of the first instances is seen in Rome's catacombs, which were originally used as burial grounds but subsequently evolved into places of pilgrimage for Christians seeking safety during periods of religious persecution. These visits were significant not just historically but also spiritually, and they revealed a profound preoccupation with one's own mortality.

However, the idea of macabre attractions has developed considerably throughout the years. This style of travel has been propelled to the forefront of the market thanks to the growth of dark tourism in the latter part of the 20th century and the early 21st century. As a result, a larger and more diverse audience is interested in participating in these kinds of adventures.

The Captivating Appeal of Sickly Delights:
Curiosity and fascination: The human capacity for curiosity is probably the single most important factor. People are naturally attracted to the mysteries and undiscovered sides of existence, particularly the shadowy and puzzling features.

Significance to History and Culture There are a lot of macabre tourist destinations that have obvious significance to either history or culture. They function as windows into the past and enable visitors to comprehend the influence that particular occurrences had on society as well as the world at large.

Emotional Resonance The serious and frequently touching nature of these attractions has a profound effect on the guests who come to see them. They provoke powerful feelings and encourage introspection on the human condition, as well as morals and society.

Education and enlightenment can be gained from visiting some of the more macabre tourist attractions. They provoke critical thought about societal issues and human behavior by illuminating intricate historical events and providing insights into such occurrences.

Unique Sensations: Some people are drawn to go to morbid attractions because they deliver unusual sensations, and this is one of the reasons why. These are the kinds of events that can be emotionally taxing, even to the point of inducing anxiety, discomfort, or catharsis.

The influence of popular culture can be seen in the prevalence of macabre themes in literature, cinema, and television. The viewing of these depictions has the potential to stimulate the attention of travelers and inspire them to seek out these locations.

In this day and age of cookie-cutter tourism and traditional vacation spots, morbid attractions provide a welcome reprieve from the mundane by providing an escape from the typical. They differentiate themselves from the typical tourist destinations by offering experiences that are one of a kind and thought provoking.

Different Categories of Disturbing Attractions:

The term "historical atrocity sites" refers to places like concentration camps, memorials to victims of genocide, and other areas associated with numerous murders. One of the most well-known examples is the concentration camp Auschwitz in Poland.

Destinations with a connection to natural or man-made disasters, such as Chernobyl in the Ukraine, provide insights into the aftermath of catastrophic occurrences including earthquakes, tsunamis, and nuclear power plant meltdowns.

Jails and Asylums: Abandoned or historic jails and mental asylums offer a peek into the legal and medical systems that were in place in the past to treat those with mental illness.

Historic battlefields, such as Gettysburg in the United States, draw visitors who are interested in the study of military history and the toll that conflict takes on its victims on a human level.

Cemeteries and Tombs: Well-known cemeteries, such as Père Lachaise in Paris, as well as catacombs in a number of different places, offer one-of-a-kind experiences that are connected to memorialization and death.

Murder & Crime Scenes: Some tourists go for locations where notorious murders took place, including the Lizzie Borden Bed and Breakfast in Massachusetts.

Locations Associated with infamous Serial Killers One subcategory of morbid attractions is made up of places that are linked to infamous serial killers such as Ted Bundy or Jeffrey Dahmer.

Museums of Medicine and Science: These types of establishments provide information on the development of medicine through displays on topics such as operations, pathology, and abnormalities in the human anatomy.

The Aspects Relating to an Individual's Psychology

A Natural Curiosity for the Macabre All humans have an innate curiosity for things that are mysterious and macabre. People are driven to investigate the more sinister sides of existence by their fascination with these topics.

Catharsis & Emotional Release: Going to macabre attractions can provide a type of catharsis and enable people to process and let go of repressed feelings or worries.

Experience Through Vicarious Means Some people are drawn to these attractions in order to experience, even vicariously, the feelings and difficulties that were experienced by those who had to live through catastrophic occurrences.

Inspiring Empathy and a Sense of Connection to the Suffering of Others Morbid attractions have been shown to inspire empathy and a sense of connection to the suffering of others, which can lead to a better knowledge of what it means to be human.

The emotional effect of these events frequently encourages people to ponder and contemplate on topics such as life and death as well as the human condition.

Considerations of an Ethical Nature:

Respect and Sensitivity: Visitors to these places are required to approach them with respect and sensitivity, bearing in mind the significance of the locations as well as the often sad events that they symbolize.

Achieving a Balance Between Education and Entertainment Educational and intellectual pursuits should take precedence over merely entertaining or sensational activities at macabre attractions.

Access and Preservation: The need to maintain the memory and dignity of the past must be balanced with the goal to give access and education. This can be accomplished by finding a happy medium between the two.

Concerns About Exploitation The commercialization of a tragedy may create concerns about the possibility of profiting from it, which may be seen as disrespectful to the memories of those who have suffered.

The Prospects for the Industry of Disturbing Attractions:

The industry is faced with a mixture of opportunities and challenges as the popularity of macabre attractions continues to rise. To maintain the authenticity and educational value of these locations, development that is both sustainable and ethical is absolutely necessary. It is imperative that responsible tourism policies be put into place to guarantee that macabre tourist destinations will continue to educate visitors about the intricacies of the human condition as well as our collective past.

There is a possibility that in the future of macabre attractions, there will be a growth in the types of locations that are visited. It is possible that modern events and experiences will become a part of the morbid appeal landscape as civilization continues to face new difficulties and crises, such as the COVID-19 epidemic. This would further underline the continuing pull of the macabre and unsettling.

4. **Purpose and scope of the book**

This book's objective is to present readers with an in-depth examination as well as a full grasp of the many facets that make up the realm of dark tourism. It seeks to dissect the intricate layers of human beings' morbid obsession with the macabre, the historical and cultural relevance of horrific sights, the ethical conundrums that come from traveling to such locations, and the ever-changing terrain of this one-of-a-kind form of tourism. Readers will obtain a thorough understanding of the relevance and impact of dark tourism on current culture as well as the travel industry if they delve deeply into the goal and scope of the book.

Having an Understanding of the Goal:

This book's major purpose is to shed light on the attraction and intricacies of dark tourism, allowing readers a balanced viewpoint on this increasingly popular and controversial form of travel. The book's secondary objective is to provide a comprehensive overview of dark tourism. It investigates the psychological, historical, and cultural components that explain the human fascination with the darker aspects of life, with the goal of addressing the interest and mystery that accompany morbid attractions. The purpose of this book is to shed light on the myriad and frequently convoluted reasons why people are interested in going to places linked with death, calamity, and the macabre by diving into the motivations of people who call themselves "dark tourists."

Additionally, the book intends to traverse the ethical landscape of dark tourism by offering a full assessment of the issues and considerations that come from the commercialization of historical suffering and tragic events. It seeks to promote a deeper understanding of the obligations of both visitors and operators in protecting the dignity and memory of the past while also ensuring that these sites continue to serve as educational and reflecting places. Its goal is to accomplish this by ensuring that these sites continue to serve as educational and reflective spaces.

Aims and Objectives of the Book:

The book goes into the cultural and historical context of the development of dark tourism, tracing its origins back to early pilgrimage locations and examining how it has evolved into the present global phenomenon that it is today. It investigates the cultural relevance of a number of macabre attractions and emphasizes the role that these attractions have in the formation of communal memory and comprehension.

Motives and Psychology: The book provides insights into the various causes behind the fascination with the macabre by exploring the psychological motives of dark tourists. These motivations range from a morbid curiosity to a morbid sense of adventure. It explores at the complex dynamic between individuals' curiosities, feelings of empathy and education, as well as the emotional experiences they've had in their lives, and their desire to travel to disturbing locations.

The book examines a wide variety of dark tourist destinations, including historical atrocity sites and disaster zones, as well as jails, asylums, and places linked with notorious personalities. These are only few of the types of dark tourism destinations that are covered in the book. It elucidates the significance of each location as well as the experiences that are available to visitors at those locations.

Ethical Considerations The ethical landscape of dark tourism is one of the primary foci of the book, which is one of its primary foci. It delves into the various issues and debates that might come from the monetization of tragedy and suffering and investigates the delicate balance that must be maintained between educating, remembering, and making money off of tragedies.

The book explores the ways in which these locations influence collective memory, shape historical narratives, and contribute to the ongoing discussion about the human experience, morality, and empathy. It also addresses the broader societal and cultural consequences of dark tourism.

The book provides insights into the future trajectory of dark tourism by conducting an analysis of recent developments and trends in the industry. It evaluates how the business may develop in reaction to societal upheavals, technological improvements, and global events. Additionally, it emphasizes the necessity of responsible and sustainable methods for maintaining the integrity of morbid attractions.

Chapter 1

The Fascination with the Macabre

The fascination with the macabre, which is both a lasting and complicated aspect of human psychology and society, has always been a source of excitement and curiosity. This fascination has been around for a very long time. This interest has its origins deep within the common human experience, and it has taken many different forms throughout the course of history, including works of art and literature, rituals, and tourism, to name the most prominent of these. This investigation dives into the complex obsession with the macabre, deconstructing its historical and cultural roots, as well as its psychological underpinnings, its manifestations in various facets of life, and its lasting attractiveness, particularly in the realm of dark tourism.

The Disturbing Continuum of History:

The fascination with the horrific and macabre has its origins far back in history. There is abundant evidence that humankind has always had a communal preoccupation with death, suffering, and the more negative aspects of existence, dating back to the first human civilizations and continuing to the present day. This part of the investigation dives into the historical development of the obsession with the macabre, highlighting how it has been expressed throughout the ages through many forms of expression, including art, literature, rituals, and cultural activities.

Observances Made in Accordance With Religious Traditions:

Through their rituals and religious practices, early human societies had a strong preoccupation with the macabre. Ancestor worship, for instance, consisted of showing respect for ancestors who had passed away, typically through the performance of rites and the presentation of offerings. In ancient Egypt, the process of mummification was an important part of the rituals that were performed to prepare the body of the departed for the afterlife. The notion that there was a hereafter and that there was a spiritual connection between the living and the dead provided the foundation for these activities.

Literature and the Arts:

Art and literature have both been effective instruments for conveying people's obsession with the macabre throughout the course of human history. The macabre was a common theme in Gothic literature, which explored topics such as death, horror, and the unknown in works such as "The Tell-Tale Heart" by Edgar Allan Poe and "Frankenstein" by Mary Shelley.

The macabre has found expression in the visual arts through the work of artists such as Francisco Goya, whose picture "The Third of May 1808" represented the horrors of war, and Hieronymus Bosch, whose fantastical paintings portrayed strange and horrific scenarios. Both of these artists are examples of artists who have contributed to the macabre.

The Afterlife in Contemporary Pop Culture:

Horror movies, television shows, and books continue to captivate viewers all over the world in our modern period, and popular culture has enthusiastically embraced this preoccupation with the macabre. It is indicative of society's ongoing preoccupation with the more sinister sides of life that the horror genre has maintained its popularity over the years. Both traditional horror films like "Psycho" and "The Shining" as well as more modern works like "The Walking Dead" have made an indelible effect on popular culture, and they continue to attract devoted fan followings to this day.

The psychological underpinnings of a morbid fascination:

The appeal of the macabre is profoundly ingrained in human psychology and reflects the intricate dynamic that exists between feelings, thoughts, and actions. This part of the article examines the psychological components of morbid curiosity in order to shed light on the reasons why humans are drawn to the darker aspects of existence.

Curiosity and awe in the face of the unknown:

The desire to know more is ingrained in us from birth, and morbid curiosity is merely an extreme form of this natural inclination. Our curiosity is frequently piqued by things that are cryptic or hidden from view. We are inherently drawn to finding secrets, whether they entail unsolved mysteries, true crime stories, or undiscovered regions. This is true whether the secrets involve known or unknown realms.

Both empathy and identification are required:

Because humans have an intrinsic propensity for empathy, we tend to have a strong attraction with macabre topics. This emotional reaction plays a crucial role in this obsession. It is possible for humans to connect with the experiences of others by engaging with narratives that involve suffering, sorrow, or death. These types of narratives can trigger deep emotional responses in listeners. In many instances, the curiosity originates from a want to comprehend, empathize with, and remember the tribulations endured by people who have been victimized.

Catharsis and release of pent-up emotions:

Participating in activities that are macabre can give a type of catharsis, enabling individuals to work through and let go of repressed feelings of fear or discomfort.

Individuals may benefit from a therapeutic outlet in the form of the profound emotional experiences linked with the macabre, which can help them come to grips with their own anxieties and phobias.

The Exhilaration of Dread:

Terror is a potent emotion, and some people are drawn to the macabre because it provides a channel through which they can experience terror in a manner that is both manageable and protected. People look for situations that will cause them to feel terrified because they find it thrilling and exhilarating, and this drives them to try to find situations that would cause them to feel scared.

Experience Gained Through Others:

The desire to live vicariously via other people is at the root of some people's obsession with macabre topics. Individuals are able to live out situations they may never have the opportunity to encounter in their own life by exploring stories or places connected with death and misery. This kind of virtual experience can be fascinating as well as emotionally compelling for the viewer.

Contemplation and Internal Processing:

The macabre has the ability to evoke strong feelings in people, which in turn often leads to introspection and thought about life, death, and the human condition. Participating in activities associated with the macabre might prompt people to reflect about existential issues, morality, and the precariousness of existence.

The macabre made manifest in the following:

The obsession with the macabre is expressed in many different facets of life, including customs and rituals, as well as art, entertainment, and tourism. In this section, we will investigate the ways in which macabre themes have permeated various aspects of human culture and society.

Travel in the Shadows:

The fascination with the macabre is made evident in a number of ways, one of which is the modern and rapidly expanding phenomena of dark tourism. Traveling to locations connected with death, misery, tragedy, or macabre themes is an example of this type of vacation. Some examples of such places are concentration camps, areas ravaged by natural disasters, decommissioned jails, and places associated with infamous people. The term "dark tourism" refers to travel that blends historical and cultural relevance with the human fascination with the most sinister sides of existence.

Literature and the Arts:

The macabre will always be expressed most effectively through the powerful mediums of art and literature. In order to attract their audiences, contemporary writers, artists, and other creators frequently rely on topics revolving around death, horror, and suffering. Contemporary graphic novels such as "From Hell" and films such as "Hereditary" investigate the more disturbing aspects of the human experience.

Theatrical Productions and Popular Culture:

The entertainment business is notorious for capitalizing on people's morbid interest in many ways. Horror media such as films, television shows, and video games provide viewers and players with an immersive experience that engages with concepts such as death, dread, and the unknown. Characters of long cultural significance, such as Freddy Krueger and Hannibal Lecter, have emerged as pop culture's go-to representatives of the macabre.

The Grim Reaper lurks in the Everyday:

The macabre can also be found in day-to-day life, such as in the variety of clothing worn by members of gothic and alternative subcultures, as well as in the rising popularity of haunted attractions and escape rooms. The gothic aesthetic has left its effect on the garment industry, as evidenced by the prevalence of black clothing, skull motifs, and other macabre themes in personal style.

Macabre fascination given a contemporary expression through the phenomenon of "dark tourism"

This continuing attractiveness can be better comprehended through the use of a fresh perspective offered by dark tourism, which is a contemporary manifestation of our preoccupation with the macabre. This part of the article digs deeper into the world of dark tourism by examining its historical roots, motivations, sorts of places, and ethical considerations.

The Historical Origins of the Dark Tourism Industry:

Even though the phrase "dark tourism" has only been around for a very short amount of time, its historical roots can be found in early pilgrimages and religious ceremonies. An early example of what is now known as "dark tourism" is found in Rome's catacombs, which were originally used as burial grounds but eventually became popular destinations for Christian pilgrims. These excursions combined piety with an investigation of the more sinister sides of life; their value lay not only in their historical but also in their religious relevance.

Reasons for Engaging in Dark Tourism:

In order to understand the attraction with the macabre, it is vital to have a solid understanding of the motivations behind dark tourism. Participating in dark tourism can be motivated by a wide variety of factors, such as an individual's natural curiosity, an interest in the region's history and culture, a desire to remember and honor the past, a pursuit of knowledge, excitement and entertainment, introspection and reflection, as well as the impact of popular culture and the media.

Different kinds of places that offer "dark tourism" are as follows:

Sites of atrocities, catastrophe zones, jails and asylums, battlefields, cemeteries and tombs, murder and crime scenes, destinations linked with serial murderers, and medical and science museums are all examples of the kind of places that fall under the umbrella term of "dark tourism." Every variety of historical site provides its visitors with their own one-of-a-kind adventures and fresh perspectives on the gruesome aspects of human history.

Considerations of an Ethical Nature Regarding Dark Tourism:

When tragedy and suffering are used for commercial gain, there is often cause for ethical concern. In order for dark tourism to be successful, participants need to demonstrate responsible behavior, sensitivity, and a commitment to protecting the memory and dignity of the past. In this line of work, one of the most persistent challenges is striking a balance between the competing imperatives of preservation and the promotion of access and education.

The Draw and Dangers of Sickly Attractions: Morbid Attractions

The preoccupation with the macabre is explored through a fresh lens when visitors go to gruesome sights, which are a subgenre of dark tourism. The appeal of these attractions, the psychological aspects that lure visitors to them, and the ethical problems that they pose are all discussed in this section of the article.

The Captivating Appeal of Sickly Delights:

Visitors are drawn in by the one-of-a-kind appeal that morbid attractions provide. They include places connected with death, suffering, and the macabre, and they frequently possess historical or cultural value. Curiosity, historical and cultural relevance, emotional resonance, education and enlightenment, distinctive sensations, the influence of pop culture, and the desire for differentiated travel experiences are some of the factors that contribute to the fascination of morbid attractions.

Attractions to the macabre from a Psychological Standpoint:

The fascination that people have with macabre themes has a lot to do with human psychology.

Individuals are drawn to these locations for a variety of reasons, including curiosity, empathy, catharsis, the thrill of dread, vicarious experience, and the opportunity for meditation and thought. These factors all play a significant influence.

Ethical Concerns Regarding Sick and Disgusting Attractions:

Ethical considerations are at the forefront of morbid attractions, just as they are with dark tourism. It is essential to strike a balance between teaching, remembering, and having fun. Visitors and those who run the sites have a responsibility to treat these locations with reverence and sensitivity, as well as a determination to protect the history of the area while maintaining access and providing education.

The Prospects for Haunted Attractions and Other Types of Spooky Tourism:

Travel destinations and forms of cultural expression are still being shaped by people's enduring preoccupation with the macabre and their attraction to ghastly attractions. This part of the article considers the possible ways in which black tourism and morbid attractions will develop in the years to come, taking into account the shifting nature of society as well as the rapid growth of technology.

Development That Is Both Sustainable And Responsible:

It is absolutely necessary to develop dark tourism and morbid attractions in a way that is both responsible and sustainable if one wishes to maintain the authenticity and educational value of these locations. The owners and managers of these attractions have a responsibility to give responsible practices, ethical considerations, and sustainability high priority as they continue to grow in popularity. This will help ensure that the past is preserved while also having a good impact on communities.

Increasing One's Perspective:

It is possible that in the future, there may be a growth in the types of locations that are visited by dark tourists. It is possible that modern occurrences and experiences, like as the COVID-19 epidemic, may become ingrained in the landscape of dark tourism. This will be a reflection of the developing interests and curiosity of tourists.

A fundamental and ever-present component of human psyche and culture is an ongoing predilection for things that are macabre. The macabre has always held a strong fascination for humans, as seen by the prevalence of ghastly themes in historical rites and religious practices, as well as in art, literature, and other contemporary forms of expression. Dark tourism and morbid attractions are contemporary representations of this obsession, and they give tourists experiences that are both distinctive and thought-provoking.

The fascination that people have with things that are morbid or gruesome stems from a combination of human traits, including empathy, curiosity, and the need for catharsis, contemplation, and emotional release. The macabre has many outlets for expression, ranging from rituals and traditions to art, literature, and popular culture. Some of these outlets are included here. Dark tourism and morbid attractions offer a contemporary lens through which one can investigate the obsession with the macabre, shedding light on the reasons why people travel, the kinds of places they go to, and the ethical issues that direct their experiences.

Opportunities and difficulties await those working in the business as a result of the continued rise in popularity of macabre tourist destinations and macabre attractions. The future of these one-of-a-kind travel experiences will be significantly influenced by factors such as responsible development, ethical considerations, and environmental sustainability. The continuing fascination of the macabre and its influence on contemporary society and culture are reflected in the ever-evolving terrain of dark tourism and morbid attractions.

1.1 Exploring the human fascination with death

The human preoccupation with morbid topics is a multifaceted and everlasting component of the human experience as a whole. It is a subject that has been investigated, questioned, and thought about throughout a wide variety of cultures, religious traditions, and historical eras. Our art, literature, rituals, and customs are all influenced by our morbid preoccupation with the hereafter. This investigation goes into the myriad facets of the human preoccupation with death, analyzing its historical and cultural origins, as well as its psychological underpinnings, manifestations in a variety of facets of life, and enduring relevance.

The Origins of Our Obsession with Death, Both Historically and Culturally

The morbid fascination that humans have always had with dying has profound historical and cultural roots that go across all of human history. The way in which humans interact with death has developed over the course of human history. These interactions have taken the form of early rituals and religious beliefs, as well as cultural behaviors and conventions. This section investigates the historical and cultural aspects of people's enduring preoccupation with death.

Observances and Beliefs Central to Religion :

Through their rituals and beliefs, early human cultures displayed a great curiosity with death. This fascination manifested itself religiously. The belief in a hereafter and the spiritual connection that was thought to exist between the living and the departed were frequently at the center of these activities. Ancestor worship, for example, consisted of showing respect for ancestors who had passed away through the performance of rites and the presentation of offerings. In ancient Egypt, the act of mummification was an important ceremony that was performed with the intention of preserving the corpse of the departed for the afterlife.

Literature and the Arts:

Art and literature have been two of the most influential outlets throughout history for expressing people's morbid interest with the hereafter. Gothic literature is characterized by its repeated preoccupation with macabre topics such as death, agony, and the unknown. These ideas are investigated in canonical works such as "The Tell-Tale Heart" by Edgar Allan Poe and "Frankenstein" by Mary Shelley, which inspire readers to ruminate on the nature of life, death, and the human condition. Artists such as Francisco Goya and Hieronymus Bosch made works in the visual arts that represent the macabre and the horrors of war. Some of these works are considered to be examples of macabre art.

Death as Practiced in Different Cultures:

Historically, various nations' cultural traditions and funeral rites have been closely intertwined with the concept of death. In many cases, the purpose of these rituals is to pay respect to those who have passed away while also giving the living a feeling of resolution. They are extremely diverse, ranging from the practice of paying respect to one's ancestors in China to the Mexican holiday known as Dia de los Muertos (Day of the Dead). The tremendous significance of death in human society is highlighted by the practices of these customs.

The Fascinating Psychology Behind Our Obsession with Death:

The attraction that humans have with death is inextricably tied to a variety of psychological processes and feelings. It expresses a complex interplay of emotions such as curiosity, empathy, dread, and a desire to comprehend the enigmas of death. In this section, the psychological aspects that lie at the root of our obsession with death will be discussed.

Curiosity and awe in the face of the unknown:

Humans are naturally inquisitive beings, and the unknown has always been something that has attracted our attention. Because of the underlying enigma and unavoidable nature of death, it is a subject that inherently piques human curiosity. Our interest with the mysterious facets of mortality is driven by the yearning to learn more about the world that exists beyond this one and the events that take place after we pass away.

Feelings of Companionship and Connection:

The profound ability for empathy that is innate to the human species undoubtedly contributes in a large way to our enduring preoccupation with mortality. Strong emotional responses might be prompted by listening to accounts of hardship, calamity, or the passing of a loved one, which can help one feel more connected to the experiences of others. The need to comprehend, empathize with, and keep in mind the fate of individuals who have endured suffering is frequently at the root of the interest.

The Pleasure of Horror for Those Who Thrill at the Macabre:

Fear is a potent emotion, and its relationship to our morbid curiosity may be traced back several generations. Individuals are drawn to the thrill of the macabre because it provides a controlled and safe method to feel dread, despite the fact that death itself can be a source of fear for them. People seek out terrifying events because they enjoy the rush of excitement and exhilaration that comes along with being terrified, and they want to feel that emotion again and again.

Catharsis and release of pent-up emotions:

Participating in activities that are macabre can give a type of catharsis, enabling individuals to work through and let go of repressed feelings of fear or discomfort. Individuals may find that the powerful emotional experiences linked with dying can serve as a therapeutic outlet, assisting them in coming to grips with their own concerns and worries in the process.

Contemplation and Internal Processing:

The morbid curiosity that people have often drives them to ruminate and think deeply about topics such as life, death, and the human condition. Existential concerns, such as those pertaining to the purpose of one's life and the nature of being human, are prompted to be pondered by individuals as a result of this. When viewed in this light, death transforms into a magnifying glass through which we investigate our own place in the wider universe.

A Fascination with the Manifestations of Death:

The preoccupation with demise can be seen expressed in many facets of modern life, including
cultural activities and rituals, art, literature, entertainment, and even travel. This section investigates how many aspects of human culture and society have been influenced by people's morbid interest with the afterlife.

Traditions and Social Practices:

The significant rituals and customs that are related with death that are practiced in many cultures are an expression of the profound obsession with mortality. Oftentimes, these rituals are means to pay respect to the departed while also bringing solace and a sense of finality to the living. The enduring significance of death in human society is reflected in the rituals that surround it, such as funerals and memorial ceremonies, as well as the construction of memorials and monuments.

Literature and the Arts:

Since the beginning of human culture, literature and the arts have been preoccupied with morbid topics related to death. Death is often used as a motif in the works of artists, writers, and other creators in order to stimulate thinking, question conventions, and engage audiences.

Whether it be through paintings, poems, or novels, the obsession with death has been a driving force in the production of some of humanity's most iconic works of art. These works have endured the test of time because of this passion.

Theatrical Productions and Popular Culture:

A prominent part that death plays in a variety of fields, including entertainment and popular culture. Many works of horror fiction, including movies, television shows, video games, and books, deal with topics such as death, dread, and the unknown. In popular culture, a fascination with death is represented by enduring symbols such as Dracula, Frankenstein's monster, and the Grim Reaper. These characters have become iconic in their own right.

The Reality of Death in Everyday Life

The human experience is not complete without a visit from death, and this reality is mirrored in many different facets of day-to-day existence. Death and the macabre can be evident in the ways in which individuals express themselves and seek out experiences that engage with these themes. This can be seen in fashion choices that include gothic and alternative subcultures, as well as in the popularity of haunted attractions and escape rooms.

A Contemporary Expression of an Age-Old Fascination with Death Tourism:

Dark tourism is a relatively new phenomena that serves as a contemporary reflection of humankind's age-old preoccupation with death. Traveling to locations connected with death, misery, tragedy, or macabre themes is an example of this type of vacation. Within this part, the historical roots, motivations, sorts of places, and ethical issues that influence dark tourism will be discussed.

The Historical Origins of the Dark Tourism Industry:

Pilgrimage destinations and ancient religious rites are the historical forebears of what is now known as the dark tourism industry. For instance, the catacombs of Rome were originally used for burials but subsequently evolved into Christian pilgrimage destinations. This allowed visitors to combine their religious devotion with an investigation of the more sinister sides of life.

Reasons for Engaging in Dark Tourism:

In order to understand the fascination with death, it is vital to have a solid understanding of the motivations underlying gloomy tourism. Participating in dark tourism can be motivated by a wide variety of factors, such as an individual's natural curiosity, an interest in the region's history and culture, a desire to remember and honor the past, a pursuit of knowledge, excitement and entertainment, introspection and reflection, as well as the impact of popular culture and the media.

Different kinds of places that offer "dark tourism" are as follows:

Sites of atrocities, catastrophe zones, jails and asylums, battlefields, cemeteries and tombs, murder and crime scenes, destinations linked with serial murderers, and medical and science museums are all examples of the kind of places that fall under the umbrella term of "dark tourism." Every variety of gravesite explores a different aspect of people's morbid preoccupation with death and the gloomier aspects of human history in its own distinctive way.

Considerations of an Ethical Nature Regarding Dark Tourism:

Concerns about ethics are frequently raised in the context of gloomy tourism due to the phenomenon of marketing of tragedy and misery. In order for dark tourism to be successful, participants need to demonstrate responsible behavior, sensitivity, and a commitment to protecting the memory and dignity of the past. In this line of work, one of the most persistent challenges is striking a balance between the competing imperatives of preservation and the promotion of access and education.

The Draw and Dangers of Sickly Attractions: Morbid Attractions:

Dark tourism, of which morbid attractions are a subgenre, presents visitors with a fresh angle from which to examine their morbid preoccupation with mortality. The appeal of these attractions, the psychological aspects that lure visitors to them, and the ethical problems that they pose are all discussed in this section of the article.

The Captivating Appeal of Sickly Delights:

Visitors are drawn in by the one-of-a-kind appeal that morbid attractions provide. They include places connected with death, suffering, and the macabre, and they frequently possess historical or cultural value. Curiosity, historical and cultural relevance, emotional resonance, education and enlightenment, distinctive sensations, the influence of pop culture, and the desire for differentiated travel experiences are some of the factors that contribute to the fascination of morbid attractions.

Attractions to the macabre from a Psychological Standpoint:

The fascination that people have with macabre themes has a lot to do with human psychology. Individuals are drawn to these locations for a variety of reasons, including curiosity, empathy, catharsis, the thrill of dread, vicarious experience, and the opportunity for meditation and thought. These factors all play a significant influence.

Ethical Concerns Regarding Sick and Disgusting Attractions:

Ethical considerations are at the forefront of morbid attractions, just as they are with dark tourism.

It is absolutely necessary to exhibit responsible behavior, sensitivity, and a commitment to the goal of conserving the memory of the past while simultaneously giving access and education. Both visitors and operators of these places have a responsibility to approach them with respect and a commitment to upholding the dignity of individuals who have endured suffering.

The Increasing Fascination With Death in the Future:
The attraction that humans have with dying is something that will always be a part of our existence, but how that fascination manifests itself in reaction to shifting power dynamics in society and advances in technology will continue to develop. This part of the article discusses the possible outcomes for death fascination in the future and how it might adjust to new conditions.

Development That Is Both Sustainable And Responsible:
It is imperative to foster the growth of dark tourism, morbid attractions, and cultural manifestations that are connected to death in a way that is both responsible and sustainable. Ethical considerations, the maintenance of the past, and the beneficial effect on communities are all vital to maintaining the authenticity of these locations and experiences.

Increasing One's Perspective:
In the not-too-distant future, the obsession with death might lead to a wider variety of tourist destinations and activities being sought out. It is possible that recent occurrences, such as the COVID-19 pandemic, will become a part of the landscape of death fascination. This will be a reflection of the developing interests and curiosities of individuals as society continues to deal with contemporary issues and crises, such as the pandemic.

The curiosity that humans have with their own mortality is diverse and has persisted throughout our existence. It has a profound presence in our past, in our society, and in our psyche, and it manifests itself in many different facets of our lives. The preoccupation with death continues to both captivate and challenge us, and it does so in a variety of ways, including rituals, art, literature, entertainment, and travel.

The psychological aspects that underlie this interest, as well as its historical and cultural roots, can shed light on the complicated relationship we have with our own demise if we have a good understanding of these aspects. The modern expressions of this obsession are known as "dark tourism" and "morbid attractions," and they provide tourists with experiences that are both distinctive and thought-provoking.

The industry is facing both opportunities and challenges as a result of the continuing rise in popularity of morbid obsession with death.

To protect the authenticity of these one-of-a-kind travel experiences and cultural expressions, it is imperative that responsible development, ethical considerations, and sustainable practices be prioritized. Our ever-evolving comprehension of life, death, and the human condition can be illuminated by the ever-changing landscape of death fascination, which is a reflection of the phenomenon's lasting significance in contemporary society and culture.

1.2 Historical perspectives on morbid curiosity

The great interest with death, misery, and other grim topics is not a recent phenomena. This is known as morbid curiosity. It has been around for a very long time, and throughout history, people have struggled with the complexity of their own curiosity about the more sinister parts of reality. This investigation digs into the historical context of morbid curiosity, charting its development throughout a variety of time periods and cultural settings.

The relationship between Ancient Civilizations and the Paranormal:

In ancient societies, beliefs in the afterlife and the supernatural were frequently the focus of morbid curiosity. The Egyptians, for instance, would embalm their dead and then construct elaborate tombs in order to guarantee that their loved ones would have a smooth journey beyond death. These ceremonies, which emphasized the significance of death as a passage to another realm, were steeped in both faith and a macabre curiosity with the hereafter.

Europe in the Middle Ages:

Macabre subject matter began to appear in works of art, works of literature, and acts of religious ritual across medieval Europe. The "Dance of Death" or the "Danse Macabre" became a famous motif that depicted a personified Death guiding people from all different walks of life to their graves. The images served as a jarring reminder of the certainty of death as well as the ethical requirements of living.

The time of the Victorians:

During the time of the Victorians, there was an increased preoccupation with mortality, which took on new forms. The culture of grieving during this time period was characterized by ornate burial rites and customs, such as the donning of apparel associated with grief and the manufacture of mourning jewelry from locks of hair taken from deceased loved ones. A preoccupation with post-mortem photography, in which deceased people were frequently photographed as a memento mori, or a reminder of mortality, was one manifestation of a morbid curiosity that presented itself as morbid curiosity.

Expressions of Cultural Identity:

The Day of the Dead celebration in Mexico and the Tibetan Sky Burials are two examples of the ways that people from different cultures have chosen to express their morbid curiosity through rituals and traditions. These practices honored and revered those who had passed away while simultaneously honoring the macabre sides of life. They made it possible for people to engage with the subject of death in a manner that was at once reverent and reflective.

The Historical Origins of "Dark Tourism":

It is possible to trace the origins of gloomy tourism, often known as the contemporary manifestation of morbid curiosity, all the way back to early pilgrimage destinations associated with death and misery. For instance, historical landmarks such as the catacombs in Rome or the Tower of London are considered to be the forerunners of modern dark tourism locations. The historical, cultural, and even macabre value of these locations was what drew tourists to these locations.

The morbid fascination with death and its mysteries has always been a fundamental component of the human experience. As a reminder of our own death and the intricacies of our fascination with the darker elements of existence, it has been conveyed through rituals, art, customs, and religious beliefs throughout human history. The historical perspectives on morbid curiosity offer some insight into how this enduring fascination has developed over time and how it has affected human society as well as people's perception of life and death.

1.3 Psychological aspects of dark tourism

The phenomena known as "dark tourism," which refers to the act of traveling to locations linked with death, misery, tragedy, and the macabre, is complex and involves a variety of psychological facets. It is possible to gain significant insights into the human fascination with the darker sides of existence by gaining an understanding of the motivations and experiences of those who participate in dark tourism.

Curiosity and awe in the face of the unknown:

Curiosity is one of the most fundamental human characteristics, and it is also one of the most important factors in dark tourism. These places have a natural air of mystery about them, and people have a natural urge to learn more about the world around them. The exploration of the tales and occurrences that have cloaked these locations in mystery and a sense of unknowability is the main draw for visitors. Visitors are drawn to these locations by their natural inquisitiveness to gain a better understanding of what took place there, how it impacted locals, and what lessons may be taken away from these events.

Feelings of Companionship and Connection:

The capacity for empathy is yet another crucially important psychological component of dark tourism. People who come to a place like this frequently try to empathize with the lives of others, particularly those who have gone through difficult times. Hearing accounts of misfortune and passing away can bring on a flood of intense feelings and help cultivate a sense of empathy in the listener. Dark tourism gives visitors the opportunity to experience a location through the eyes of those who were there at the time of a traumatic occurrence or who were personally impacted by it. This connection is one of the primary motivating factors behind people's interest in macabre topics.

Catharsis and release of pent-up emotions:

The emotional intensity of travel experiences that are considered to fall under the category of "dark tourism" can sometimes act as a type of catharsis. These interactions may serve as a therapeutic outlet for visitors, enabling them to work through and let go of repressed feelings of anxiety or anger. Some people find that experiencing the profound emotions that are linked with these sites provides them with a sense of release and a sense of completion.

The Exhilaration of Dread:

Fear is a potent emotion, and there are some people who find that they enjoy the rush that

comes from macabre entertainment. Visiting a haunted attraction can frequently provide a controlled and secure feeling of fear and anxiety. People come here to have these kinds of adventures so they may feel the thrill and excitement that comes from facing one's fears and putting oneself in uncomfortable situations. It is possible for it to be a type of contained enthusiasm in which people voluntarily choose to participate.

Experience Gained Through Others:

Some people find that participating in dark tourism gives them the opportunity to live out experiences that they may never actually have in their own life. It gives people the opportunity to investigate narratives and locations connected with death and pain without actually forcing them to confront these things in their own lives. The macabre attractions provide a medium through which visitors can have vicarious experiences that are not only fascinating but also emotionally compelling.

Contemplation and Internal Processing:

The fascination with the macabre frequently prompts people to contemplate and ruminate on topics such as life and death as well as the human condition. Visitors are encouraged to reflect on existential issues, issues of morality, and the precariousness of existence while they are there. Individuals are encouraged to engage in introspection as well as philosophical contemplation about the human experience as well as the repercussions of our acts when they participate in dark tourism.

The psychological components of dark tourism provide a comprehensive understanding of the motives that motivate individuals to engage with the venues that are included in this type of tourism. The intricate nature of our fixation on the more disturbing aspects of life is shed light on by the interaction of factors such as curiosity, empathy, catharsis, the rush of dread, vicarious experience, and the chance for thought and contemplation. Dark tourism gives a novel perspective from which to investigate these psychological characteristics and provides a profound understanding of the human mind as well as the complex relationship that the human mind has with death, misery, and the macabre.

1.4 Contemporary drivers of interest in the macabre

In today's society, the human psyche continues to be captivated and tested by a fascination with the macabre despite the many advances in medical science. While historical and psychological considerations give a foundation for understanding this fascination, contemporary society introduces new and growing drivers that fuel our interest about the darker sides of existence. Despite this, we continue to be fascinated by these topics. This investigation dives into the modern-day forces that are responsible for people's fascination with the macabre, shedding light on the shifting terrain of people's preoccupation with death, misery, and the macabre.

The Role of Contemporary Media in Having an Effect:

The proliferation of modern media in this age of information technology is a significant contributor to the escalation of our interest in macabre topics. There is a plethora of content that can be found in various mediums, such as television, film, literature, and the internet, that investigates topics such as death, dread, and the unknown. The modern media industry understands our intrinsic need for excitement and satisfies it in a variety of forms, including but not limited to immersive video games, true crime documentaries, horror films, and podcasts. The convenience with which we may acquire this stuff has helped to normalize our preoccupation with the macabre, thereby establishing it as an essential component of the entertainment culture that we have developed.

Actual Offenses Committed and Mysteries Yet to be Resolved:

In recent years, true crime shows have become one of the most popular contemporary drivers of morbid curiosity. The investigation of real-life murders and unsolved puzzles is a topic that has been explored in popular media such as the podcast "Serial," the television series "Making a Murderer," and books such as "In Cold Blood." Our interest in these tales is driven by our insatiable curiosity regarding the inner workings of criminal minds, the intricacies of the judicial system, and the depths to which humans are capable of falling. People are particularly drawn to mysteries that have not yet been solved because they harbor the desire to solve the mystery and learn the truth.

The Relationship Between Social Media and Online Communities:

People who share similar interests have been able to connect with one another more easily thanks to social media and online groups. These platforms offer areas for sharing, discussing, and investigating macabre topics, which may be accessed by users. Subreddits, YouTube channels, and Facebook groups that are oriented on paranormal investigations have become hubs for individuals to express their fascination with the darker elements of existence. These subreddits, YouTube channels, and Facebook groups are all devoted to visiting haunted sites and investigating the paranormal. These online forums encourage a sense of connection and a common interest, which contributes to a further increase in the obsession with macabre topics.

Tourism in the Dark and Other Disturbing Attractions:

Dark tourism is a relatively new concept that has seen tremendous growth in popularity over the past few years. It entails going to locations connected with death, pain, tragedy, and other themes related with the macabre. Dark tourism locations may be found all over the world, from Auschwitz in Poland to Alcatraz Island in the United States. These destinations provide visitors with one-of-a-kind and thought-provoking experiences. The attractiveness of these locations resides in their historical, cultural, and emotional value. They entice tourists with the promise of dealing with the most disturbing aspects of human history, which contributes to their popularity.

The Investigation of the Supernatural and the Paranormal:
The modern world's preoccupation with the unexplained and the paranormal is another factor that contributes to the rise in popularity of macabre topics. Television shows such as "Ghost Adventures" and "Paranormal Witness" present studies of haunted locales and encounters with the unexplained on their screens. People are driven to interact with the macabre in their search for answers to questions about the afterlife, the afterlife itself, and the supernatural world in general because of their desire to investigate the possibility of an afterlife, speak with spirits, and learn the secrets of the supernatural world.

Popular culture and the aesthetics of the dark:
It is impossible to overlook the impact that popular culture has had, as well as the rising popularity of gothic aesthetics. The gothic and alternative subcultures have flourished thanks to the proliferation of fashion options that feature gothic and macabre motifs, as well as black apparel and skull designs. This preoccupation with gloomy aesthetics extends beyond the realm of fashion and into other creative fields such as music, art, and literature. Artists like Tim Burton and bands like Marilyn Manson are revered for their study of the macabre, and their work has had a significant impact on modern culture and aesthetics.

The Exhilaration of Fear and Complete Immersion in an Experience:
Significant forces that contribute to our modern fascination in the macabre are the thrill of terror and experiences that immerse us in the encounter. People get the chance to face their fears in a setting that is both controlled and secure when they participate in interactive horror experiences like haunted attractions, escape rooms, and other such activities. These events stimulate our most basic instincts and provide the adrenaline rush that comes from facing our fears and venturing into the unknown.

Consideration Given to the Human Predicament:
The modern fascination with death sometimes includes a need to reflect on the human condition, which is despite the fact that the macabre has always held a certain charm. Individuals are prompted to contemplate existential concerns, morality, and the precarious nature of life when they investigate topics such as suffering, mortality, and the more negative aspects of existence. This kind of introspection is a driving factor behind the fascination with the macabre, and it serves as a means of coming to grips with our own existence so that we can have a better knowledge of it.

Our modern culture has introduced new and ever-evolving drivers that fuel our interest with the macabre, and these drivers have contributed to its development. Our interest in the darker aspects of existence has been normalized and amplified thanks to the influence of modern media, true crime, online communities, dark tourism, the exploration of the supernatural, dark aesthetics, immersive experiences, and a reflection on the human condition. All of these factors have contributed to the normalization of our interest in these aspects of existence. It is becoming increasingly clear that this enduring allure is a complex and multifaceted aspect of the human experience as these current factors continue to influence the terrain of interest with the macabre.

Chapter 2

Dark Tourism Through the Ages

The concept of "dark tourism," which refers to the act of traveling to locations linked with death, misery, tragedy, and the macabre, is a multifaceted phenomena that has developed over the course of human history. Dark tourism provides a perspective through which to explore humanity's continuous interest with the darker parts of existence. Its early roots may be traced back to religious pilgrimages, and modern explorations of war memorials, haunted locales, and crime scenes are all examples of dark tourism's contemporary manifestations. This investigation takes us on a voyage through time, diving into the historical growth of dark tourism, analyzing its motivations, types of places, and ethical considerations, as well as contemplating its position in the present world.

Pilgrimage and other forms of religious tourism had their beginnings in ancient times

It is possible to trace the origins of dark tourism all the way back to religious pilgrimages and ceremonies that were centered around locations significant for their association with death, martyrs, and the spiritual. These early manifestations of curiosity with the macabre were strongly founded in religious ideas and functioned as a means of connecting with the holy while investigating the darker parts of existence. These expressions of fascination with the macabre can be found all over the world.

Journeys to the Sites of the Martyrs' Shrines:

Pilgrimages to the shrines of martyrs are sometimes cited as one of the earliest examples of what is now known as "dark tourism." In the early days of Christianity, for instance, the catacombs of Rome were used as burial grounds; with time, however, they evolved into pilgrimage destinations for Christians. The first followers of Christianity traveled to the catacombs to pay their respects to the martyrs, strengthen their connection to their religion, and gain insight into the more difficult elements of life via their devotion to those who had suffered for their beliefs.

Observances of Religion Prior to Death:

Throughout the course of human history, many different religious groups have embraced rites and activities connected to the afterlife. One such example is the practice of relic veneration, which entailed the protection and presentation of the relics of holy people such as martyrs and saints. These relics were kept in elaborate shrines that were located inside of churches and cathedrals. They were revered because they provided a direct link to the divine.

The Mourning Culture and the Development of Cemeteries During the Victorian Era

A key transitional stage in the history of the development of dark tourism was during the Victorian era. The culture of sorrow, the traditions surrounding funerals, and the development of cemeteries all played a significant part in the preoccupation with death throughout this time period. The distinctive practices and ceremonies of that era were distinguished by the ornate and macabre ways in which they expressed sorrow and loss.

The Culture of Mourning

The public show of sadness and loss was a significant component of Victorian mourning culture. People were expected to dress in mourning garb, which typically consisted of dark clothing and symbolic ornaments like mourning brooches and lockets containing the deceased person's hair. As a prominent means of expressing sadness and as a subgenre of gloomy tourism, the production of mourning jewelry, which was made from materials such as jet and onyx, became popular.

The Movement for the Garden Cemetery:

During the Victorian era, garden cemeteries, which are often referred to as country cemetery, came into existence. These cemeteries were intended to be places of reflection and recollection, therefore they were planned to be gorgeous and peaceful. This movement can be seen most prominently in cemeteries such as Highgate Cemetery in London and Père Lachaise Cemetery in Paris. People went to these cemeteries not only to pay their respects to the people who had passed away, but also to admire the artwork, architecture, and symbolism that were incorporated into the graves and memorials.

War Memorials and Places of Genocide are Examples of Historical "Dark Tourism"

The 20th century witnessed considerable advancements in the field of dark tourism, notably in the wake of great wars and crimes that took place throughout the century. Important sites for remembering the evil side of history and learning more about it have emerged as places linked with World Wars I and II, the Holocaust, and other crimes.

The Battlefields of World War I:

Early examples of historical "dark tourism" can be seen at the battlefields of World War I, such as the Somme in France. People traveled to these battlefields to learn about the brutal reality of trench warfare and to pay their respects to the troops who lost their lives fighting there. In order to provide historical context and interpretation, museums and memorials were built all over the world.

Memorials to Holocaust Victims and Former Concentration Camps:

In the annals of grim tourism, the Holocaust is remembered as one of the most pivotal events that ever took place. Concentration camps such as Auschwitz and Dachau have evolved into sites of memorialization, education, and introspection in recent decades. People from all over the world travel to these locations to confront the atrocities of the Holocaust, educate themselves on its history, and pay their respects to those who were murdered during the Holocaust.

The Development of Modern Nighttime Tourism

Although it has strong historical roots, dark tourism did not enjoy a considerable spike in popularity until the latter half of the 20th century, and it is still developing in the 21st century. The modern conception of what is known as "dark tourism" comprises a wide variety of locations, reasons for going, and ethical factors to think about.

Different kinds of places that offer "dark tourism" are as follows:

Locations that are known to be associated with massive acts of violence and suffering, such as the Killing Fields in Cambodia and the Ground Zero Memorial in New York City. Sites of atrocity include both of these places.

Calamity Zones are regions that have been impacted by a natural or man-made calamity, such as the nuclear power plant at Chernobyl in the Ukraine or the ancient city of Pompeii in Italy.

Prisons and Asylums: Former prisons and mental asylums, such as the Trans-Allegheny Lunatic Asylum in West Virginia and Alcatraz Island in California. Both of these locations are in the United States.

Historic battlegrounds, including places like Gettysburg in the United States and Gallipoli in Turkey, are referred to as battlefields.

Cemeteries and Tombs: Some of the most well-known cemeteries and tombs in the world are located in Paris, including Père Lachaise and the Catacombs.

Sites that are associated with infamous murders and crimes, such as the Lizzie Borden House in Massachusetts and the Whitechapel district in London, are referred to as "murder and crime scenes."

Places that have a connection to the lives and crimes of serial killers, such as the murder sites associated with Ted Bundy and the apartment that Jeffrey Dahmer rented in Milwaukee are examples of locations associated with serial killers.

Institutions such as the Mutter Museum in Philadelphia and the Museum of Broken Relationships in Croatia are examples of museums that display artifacts linked to the history of medicine, surgery, and scientific exploration. Medical and science museums are also known as historical medical and scientific museums.

Reasons for Engaging in Dark Tourism:

Curiosity can be defined as the desire to learn about new things and uncover hidden stories from the past.

A Sincere Interest in Understanding the Site's Historical and Cultural Significance A sincere interest in comprehending the historical and cultural significance of the places.

Remembering and respecting individuals who have suffered or passed away at these areas is necessary in order to show proper remembrance and respect.

Education can be defined as the pursuit of information and a more in-depth comprehension of past occurrences.

The appeal of experiencing fear, excitement, and the unknown in a controlled atmosphere is what we mean when we talk about thrill and entertainment.

A place for individuals to go to think deeply and reflectively about life, death, and the human condition is provided by Reflection and Contemplation.

The impact of works of literature, films, television series, and documentaries that deal with macabre subjects are examples of this type of cultural influence.

Considerations of an Ethical Nature Regarding Dark Tourism:

Concerns about ethics are frequently raised in the context of gloomy tourism due to the phenomenon of marketing of tragedy and misery. In order for dark tourism to be successful, participants need to demonstrate responsible behavior, sensitivity, and a commitment to protecting the memory and dignity of the past. In this line of work, one of the most persistent challenges is striking a balance between the competing imperatives of preservation and the promotion of access and education.

Dark Tourism Contains One Particular Type Called Morbid Attractions.

Dark tourism, of which morbid attractions are a subgenre, presents visitors with a fresh angle from which to examine their morbid preoccupation with mortality. These tourist destinations include places connected with death, misery, and the macabre, and they frequently retain historical or cultural significance. Curiosity, historical and cultural relevance, emotional resonance, education and enlightenment, distinctive sensations, the influence of pop culture, and the desire for differentiated travel experiences are some of the factors that contribute to the fascination of morbid attractions.

The Captivating Appeal of Sickly Delights:

Visitors are drawn in by the one-of-a-kind appeal that morbid attractions provide. They include places connected with death, suffering, and the macabre, and they frequently possess historical or cultural value. Curiosity, historical and cultural relevance, emotional resonance, education and enlightenment, distinctive sensations, the influence of pop culture, and the desire for differentiated travel experiences are some of the factors that contribute to the fascination of morbid attractions.

Attractions to the macabre from a Psychological Standpoint:

The fascination that people have with macabre themes has a lot to do with human psychology. Individuals are drawn to these locations for a variety of reasons, including curiosity, empathy, catharsis, the thrill of dread, vicarious experience, and the opportunity for meditation and thought. These factors all play a significant influence.

Ethical Concerns Regarding Sick and Disgusting Attractions:

Ethical considerations are at the forefront of morbid attractions, just as they are with dark tourism. It is absolutely necessary to exhibit responsible behavior, sensitivity, and a commitment to the goal of conserving the memory of the past while simultaneously giving access and education. Both visitors and operators of these places have a responsibility to approach them with respect and a commitment to upholding the dignity of individuals who have endured suffering.

The Prospects for Haunted Attractions and Other Types of Spooky Tourism:
The future of macabre tourism and macabre attractions is set to be filled with opportunities as well as obstacles. To protect the authenticity of these one-of-a-kind travel experiences and cultural expressions, it is imperative that responsible development, ethical considerations, and sustainable practices be prioritized. The ever-changing panorama of dark tourism and morbid attractions is illuminating for our continuously developing comprehension of life, death, and the human condition because it demonstrates the lasting significance of these phenomena in contemporary society and culture.

The human preoccupation with the more macabre sides of life is revealed in a fresh and fascinating light through the phenomenon of "dark tourism" and "morbid attractions." These behaviors and venues have developed over time in reaction to changes in cultural norms, historical norms, and technical norms. Their origins can be traced back to religious pilgrimages, but their modern manifestations are quite different. They continue to enthrall people and put them in uncomfortable situations, and as a result, they provide us new perspectives on the complicated relationship we have with death, misery, and the macabre. We acquire a deeper appreciation for the ongoing fascination of these behaviors and their presence in the modern world when we obtain an awareness of the motivations, types of places, and ethical considerations involved with dark tourism and morbid attractions.

2.1 Historical roots of dark tourism

Dark tourism, which involves going to places linked with death, tragedy, and the macabre, has profound historical origins that may be traced back through the centuries-long history of human civilization. The historical roots of dark tourism demonstrate humanity's continuous fascination with the most sinister facets of existence. These roots can be traced back to early pilgrimage sites and religious rites, as well as the commemoration of historical events and the investigation of human misery. This investigation goes into the historical foundations of dark tourism, analyzing its early manifestations, cultural expressions, and theological significance, and offering light on the ways in which these roots continue to impact contemporary behaviors and attitudes in the tourism industry today.

Earlier Forms of Religious Travel and Practices:
It is possible to trace the historical roots of dark tourism back to early pilgrimages and religious ceremonies that were concentrated around locations of martyrs, religious significance, and spiritual devotion. These locations were known as "dark tourism

hotspots." People in ancient civilizations went on pilgrimages to holy sites, which were frequently associated with the enduring of hardships, the performing of sacrifices, and the attainment of enlightenment. Through religious devotion and appreciation for those who had suffered for their religion, these pilgrimages functioned as a means of connecting with the divine and investigating the darker parts of human existence. This was accomplished by traveling to sacred sites.

The Worship of Relics and Their Spiritual Connections:

The tradition of relic veneration, in which the remains of saints and martyrs were preserved and shown, is an additional significant component of the historical foundations of dark tourism. This practice involved the protection and presentation of relics. During the time period known as the Middle Ages, religious buildings such as cathedrals and monasteries were known to store relics that were thought to possess spiritual qualities and connections to the divine. Pilgrims would travel enormous distances to view these relics in the hopes of gaining some sort of spiritual peace, physical healing, and a deeper comprehension of the mysteries that surround life and death.

Culture of Mourning and the Victorian Obsession with Death:

The Victorian era was a pivotal time in the development of dark tourism, which was defined by a macabre preoccupation with death and elaborate mourning rituals. This era was a crucial milestone in the history of dark tourism. The culture of mourning during this time period was distinguished by its ornate demonstrations of sadness. Mourning dress, mourning jewelry, and practices that stressed public displays of sorrow and remembering were commonplace throughout this time period. This time period witnessed the development of garden cemeteries, which became popular places for people to go to pay their respects to deceased loved ones and engage in meditative activities, further reinforcing the cultural connection between death, remembrance, and the human obsession with the afterlife.

Memorials to Veterans and Other Places of Remembrance:

The remembrance of historical events, particularly those connected with conflict, has also played an important influence in the development of the historical origins of dark tourism. Individuals have been drawn to the sites of major conflicts throughout history, from the battlefields of the ancient world to the sites of World War I and World War II, in order to pay their respects to the dead, honor the memory of those who have sacrificed their lives, and gain a deeper understanding of the human cost of war. These conflicts included World War I and World War II. Many memorials and commemoration places have been established all over the world to serve as sobering reminders of the horrors of war and the enduring impact that human suffering has had.

Historical Tragedies and Expressions of Cultural Identity:

There have been many different cultural manifestations that have come into existence over the

course of history to represent humanity's obsession with historical tragedies and the more negative aspects of being alive. Culture has always been a means by which people have attempted to come to terms with the difficulties of mortality, sadness, and the precarious nature of existence. Examples of this include everything from ancient theatrical performances based around themes of death and suffering to literary works that explore the human condition.

These creative representations have made a contribution to the formation of social views about death and the macabre, thereby laying the framework for the contemporary preoccupation with dark tourism.

Locations of Worship and Other Sacred Places:

Religious buildings and other types of sacred spaces have, for a very long time, been linked to the more negative aspects of human existence because of their function as locations for spiritual reflection, reverence, and contemplation. These locations, which range from ancient temples and shrines to medieval cathedrals and monasteries, have offered people opportunities for spiritual connection, pilgrimage, and encounters with the secrets of the divine throughout history. They have also functioned as repositories of cultural and historical value, maintaining the memory of saints, religious leaders, and events that have shaped religious traditions and beliefs. In other words, they have played an important role in the preservation of religious history.

Cultural Observances and Ancestral Remembrance Practices:

The historical foundations of dark tourism have been significantly influenced by a variety of cultural practices and commemorative rituals during the course of its development. Cultures all over the world have established their own one-of-a-kind ways of paying respect to the gone, remembering those who have passed away, and acknowledging the effect that death has on the living. These practices range from ancient burial rituals and grieving traditions to contemporary memorial services and commemorative events. These rituals have helped to establish cultural narratives concerning death and the afterlife, which in turn has contributed to the development of a sense of continuity and connection between generations of the past and the present.

The Earliest Attempts to Explain the Supernatural:

The investigation of the paranormal and the unfathomable is another important component that has played a key role in the development of dark tourism's historical roots. Ancient civilizations and medieval communities frequently engaged in rites and rituals with the goals of better comprehending the enigmas of the afterlife, establishing communication with the spirit world, and deciphering the mysteries of the unknown. research of the supernatural has resulted in a complex tapestry of narratives that reflect humanity's everlasting interest with the mysteries of life and death. These narratives range from ancient divination practices and spiritualist traditions to medieval tales of ghostly meetings and spectral apparitions. These tales are all a result of humanity's research of the supernatural.

The historical origins of dark tourism provide light on the intricate and multidimensional nature of the connection that exists between human culture, spirituality, and the more sinister parts of being alive. The persistent human interest with the mysteries of mortality, the hereafter, and the unknown may be seen reflected in the historical development of gloomy tourism.

This attraction manifested itself in the form of early pilgrimages and religious rites, as well as in the commemoration of historical events and the examination of human misery. These historical origins continue to impact modern views and practices concerning death, remembrance, and the macabre, highlighting the ever-present significance of dark tourism in the overall scope of the human experience.

2.2 Early examples of morbid attractions

The history of macabre attractions, which are a subcategory of dark tourism, is deeply rooted and spans multiple epochs, cultures, and civilizations. The grisly spectacles of ancient Rome and the medieval relics of saints and martyrs are two early instances of morbid attractions that demonstrate humanity's everlasting interest with the darkest parts of existence. Both of these examples are from the medieval period. This investigation digs into the historical roots of macabre attractions, analyzing the myriad ways in which they have manifested themselves, as well as the myriad ways in which they have influenced contemporary activities.

Gladiatorial Combat and the Practice of Public Executions in Ancient Rome

Some of the earliest and most vivid examples of morbid attractions are found in ancient Rome's

spectacular shows, which date back to the city's early days. In particular, the Roman Colosseum served as a center for macabre entertainment. Tens of thousands of people would assemble there to watch gladiator fights, public executions, and hunts for wild animals. The spectacle of these events was a large part of their appeal, as was the chance to observe fights to the death in a setting that was safe and secure for spectators.

Battles of the Gladiators:

Competitions between gladiators were an integral part of Roman culture and entertainment. These battles took place in grandiose arenas such as the Colosseum and pitted trained gladiators against one another, frequently to the point of death. The sight of violence and death had a sickening attraction for viewers as they watched the contestants engage with various weapons. Crowds flocked to see the combatants battle with various weapons.

Assassinations in Public:

Another source of morbid curiosity in ancient Rome was the public execution of criminals and political opponents. These events were frequently carried out with elaborate and horrific rites, the purpose of which was to communicate messages of authority and justice to the participants. Large audiences would gather to watch grisly spectacles such as public executions because they were used both as a kind of entertainment and as a method of meting out punishment.

Pilgrimages and Artifacts from the Middle Ages

The Middle Ages saw a new form of macabre fascination emerge: the adoration of relics, particularly those connected to saints and martyrs. This was a form of morbid attraction that had not been seen before. Relics were objects of attraction and devotion due to the widespread belief that they have spiritual importance as well as the ability to perform miracles. Pilgrims would travel to various holy locations in order to show their respect for various relics and to look for comfort on a spiritual level.

The Honoring of Relics:
The practice of adoration of relics entailed the protection and presentation of the remains of holy people, martyrs, or other important characters in religious history. Ornate reliquaries, which were complex vessels designed to keep and show the relics, were frequently employed to store these remains. Reliquaries are sometimes known as reliquaries. Pilgrims had the belief that these relics possessed the power to provide protection, healing, and a connection to a higher spiritual power.

Pilgrimages for Religious Purposes:
During the medieval era, pilgrimages to locations that were associated with relics became increasingly popular. Pilgrims would travel great distances in order to see cathedrals, churches, and shrines that housed holy relics and artifacts. The actual voyage was frequently difficult and laden with peril, but the allure of meeting the sacred and establishing a more profound connection with the divine inspired many people to set out on these expeditions.

Europe in the Middle Ages: Dancing with Death
A passionate and grotesque display of morbid fascination, the "Dance of Death" or "Danse Macabre" was popular in medieval Europe. This artistic motif depicted a personified version of Death ushering individuals from a wide variety of walks of life into the hereafter. The artwork drew attention to the fact that death is unavoidable and the importance of living a morally responsible life.

Manifestation of the Arts:
The "Dance of Death" was a popular motif in medieval art and literature, and it may be found depicted in a variety of mediums, including paintings, woodcuts, and written works. It frequently showed Death as a skeletal figure, escorting members of varying social levels, including kings, nobles, peasants, and clergy, to their final resting places. These pictures were created with the intention of serving as reminders of one's own death and the common end that was in store for everyone.

Reflection on Ethical and Philosophical Issues:
The song "Dance of Death" inspired individuals to reflect on the fleeting nature of life and the ethical obligations that come with being an individual. It drove home the point that death was the great equalizer, in that it claimed both the powerful and the powerless in equal measure. This gloomy contemplation on one's own demise was a major undercurrent running through the culture of the time.

The Victorian Era: Mourning Culture and the Beginnings of Photography as a Memorial
Mourning culture and memorial photography gave rise to a novel type of macabre fascination during the Victorian era. This trend continued well into the 20th century.

This time period was distinguished by the performance of elaborate mourning rituals, the wearing of mourning clothes, and the manufacture of mourning jewelry that incorporated locks of hair taken from deceased loved ones.

The Culture of Mourning

The Victorian culture of mourning was distinguished by the rigid protocols that were expected of those expressing their sorrow. The bereaved were supposed to dress in mourning apparel, which consisted of dark clothing and accessories, for a predetermined amount of time after the passing of a loved one. People were encouraged to show their sorrow in public as part of the culture of mourning, which also served as a forum in which they could remember the departed and pay their respects to the deceased.

Photographs of Memorial Services:

The taking of memorial photographs was a common activity throughout the Victorian era of mourning, and it was one of the most notable aspects of this period. During a period when photography was becoming more and more popular, families would often have post-mortem photographs taken of deceased members of their family. These images, which were frequently posed to look as though they were taken recently, served as mementos and reminders of the person who had passed away. This practice was a sort of morbid attraction in which commemoration and a fascination with death were blended into a single activity.

The Development of Medical Museums and Collections of Unique Objects

The nineteenth century saw the proliferation of medical museums and cabinets of curiosities, which displayed anatomical specimens, medical anomalies, and pathological abnormalities. These museums and exhibitions attracted interested guests who were fascinated by macabre topics and the mysteries of the human body.

Museum of the Anatomy and Physiology of Disease:

The Museum of Pathological Anatomy in Vienna, Austria, was established in 1796 and is a remarkable example of this type of institution. This museum has an extensive collection of preserved anatomical specimens, which included organs, skeletons, and pathological preparations among other things. The exhibitions, which provided insights into medical research, anatomy, and the implications of disease, drew visitors in for the purpose of exploration.

Display Cases Filled with Oddities:

Cabinets of curiosities, also known as Wunderkammern, were collections of strange and odd things that included wonders from the natural world, art, science, and the macabre. These collections were often displayed in elaborate rooms called Wunderkammern. These cabinets were frequently held by members of the nobility and provided visitors with sources of amazement and interest during their time there. They included specimens such as unusual minerals, taxidermied creatures, and antiques from faraway locations. In addition, they included items that had characteristics that were macabre or horrific.

These early examples of horrific attractions offer a look into the varied and everlasting nature of humankind's interest with the macabre due to the fact that they date back to ancient times. The gruesome spectacles of ancient Rome, the veneration of relics in the Middle Ages, the "Dance of Death" in medieval Europe, the mourning culture of Victorian England, and the development of medical museums and curiosities are some examples of how morbid attractions have developed over time and manifested themselves in different ways across a variety of historical periods and cultural contexts. The roots of morbid attractions continue to impact contemporary practices and attitudes, revealing the delicate relationship that exists between the things that fascinate people and the more disturbing aspects of life.

2.3 Transformation and evolution over time

The concept of morbid attractions,' which is a subset of 'dark tourism,' has seen substantial change and development over the course of history. The idea of morbid attractions has consistently evolved to the shifting cultural, societal, and technical landscapes ever since its early roots can be traced back to horrible spectacles and religious practices. More recently, medical museums and contemporary forms of ghastly fascination have joined the ranks of the concept of morbid attractions. This investigation traces the emergence and modification of macabre attractions over the course of time, offering insight on their historical progression, cultural expressions, and the enduring fascination that continues to captivate audiences in the present era.

From Ancient Rome to Medieval Europe: An Overview of the First Religious Celebrations and Rituals

Spectacular Displays of Morbidity in Ancient Rome

In ancient Rome, horrible events like as gladiatorial combat and public executions drew large crowds. These early kinds of morbid attractions may be observed in ancient Rome. These shows were notable for the brutality, bloodshed, and the adrenaline-pumping experience of viewing fights to the death that they featured. The attractiveness of such events was based on the spectacle itself because they offered the public a controlled atmosphere in which to enjoy macabre activities.

Relics, Pilgrimages, and the "Dance of Death" in Medieval Europe.

In medieval Europe, morbid attractions took on a new shape, revolving around the worship of relics, religious pilgrimages, and a practice known as the "Dance of Death." The practice of adoration of relics included the act of preserving and exhibiting the remains of holy people and martyrs who were considered to hold spiritual importance and the potential to perform miracles. Pilgrims set out on treks to various holy sites in order to show their reverence for various relics and to look for a connection to their spiritual selves.

The "Dance of Death" was a motif in art that stressed the unavoidability of death as well as the importance of adhering to moral precepts. It depicted a personified version of Death bringing people from a variety of social classes to their graves, prompting introspection about the fleeting nature of life and the moral obligations of humans.

The Mourning Culture of the Victorian Era and the Development of Memorial Photography

Mourning culture and memorial photography gave rise to a novel type of macabre fascination throughout the Victorian era. This development occurred during that time period. This time was marked by elaborate rituals of grieving, the donning of apparel appropriate for the occasion, and the making of memorial images of deceased loved ones. Mourning culture placed an emphasis on the public show of mourning and offered individuals a channel through which they could communicate their sadness and honor the memory of the departed.

The practice of memorial photography in particular stands out as an example of a sort of morbid attraction that blended remembering the deceased with an obsession with death. As mementos and recollections of the deceased, families would have post-mortem photographs taken of their deceased loved ones, with the photos often being staged to look as though they were still alive.

Medical Museums and Other Curiosities from the 19th Century

The nineteenth century saw the growth of medical museums and cabinets of curiosities, which displayed anatomical specimens, medical anomalies, and pathological abnormalities. Visitors were given insights into medical science, anatomy, and the effects of sickness by visiting institutions and exhibitions such as the Museum of Pathological Anatomy in Vienna, Austria. Other institutions and exhibitions gave similar opportunities. These museums acted as a kind of macabre attraction, drawing in those who were fascinated about the macabre and intrigued by the wonders of the human body.

Cabinets of curiosities, also known as Wunderkammern, became increasingly popular during this time period. These were essentially collections of strange and unique artifacts, and they included gruesome objects as well as wonders from the natural world, art, and science. These cabinets held a variety of objects, including unusual minerals, taxidermied animals, and artifacts that had a macabre or macabre-like quality to them.

The 20th Century: A Decade of True Crime and Haunted Attractions

The 20th century witnessed the rise of a number of noteworthy examples of morbid attractions, including dark tourism and the obsession with real-life crimes.

Travel in the Shadows:

The term "dark tourism," which was first used in the 1990s, refers to the practice of traveling to locations that are linked with death, pain, tragedy, and the macabre. It comprises a diverse range of locations, including memorials to war and concentration camps, as well as zones afflicted by natural disasters and places associated with infamous crimes. The more sinister sides of human history and culture can be discovered by visitors to these locations, which provide that possibility.

The Real Story:

The 20th and 21st centuries have seen a huge increase in people's attention with actual criminal cases. Real-life mysteries and crimes have become a popular subject for documentaries, podcasts, books, and even television shows. This popularity has also spread to audiobooks. Audiences are drawn to these narratives because of the need to gain insight into the motivations of criminals, the complexity of the judicial system, and the potential for evil that exists within human nature.

The Morbid Attractions of the Modern World in the Age of Digital Technology

The internet's ability to connect people all over the world and the abundance of content that delves into the macabre have both contributed to an expansion of the meaning of the term "morbid attractions" in the modern era. The evolution of the internet has made it possible for individuals to connect with their morbid interest through a variety of new mediums. These mediums include online groups that discuss real-life crimes and unsolved mysteries, as well as websites devoted to the supernatural and paranormal.

Communities found on the Internet:

Online communities that are oriented on macabre attractions have emerged thanks to the proliferation of social media platforms, forums, and dedicated websites. These platforms provide places where people who hold similar perspectives can gather to communicate, discuss, and investigate the more negative aspects of existence. Subreddits devoted to true crime, YouTube channels focusing on haunted locales, and Facebook groups centered on paranormal investigations have become hubs for individuals to express their curiosity with macabre topics and topics related to the paranormal.

Production of Content:

The proliferation of digital material creation has led to an increased interest in macabre tourist destinations. Macabre material is produced by individuals and creators, and can take the form of blogs, podcasts, YouTube videos, and even virtual reality experiences that dive into the subject matter. A larger audience will be able to connect with the more difficult parts of life and history thanks to the content in question.

A Look at Some Ethical Concerns Regarding Sick Attractions

The development of macabre attractions has not taken place in a vacuum free of ethical considerations. Engaging with morbid attractions requires a commitment to responsible behavior, empathy, and the preservation of the memory and dignity of the past. This is especially important given the rise in the commercialization of tragedy and pain.

Behavior that is Responsible:

The visitors of morbid attractions are expected to treat these places with the appropriate amount of respect and responsibility. The memory of the past can be sullied not just by disruptive or disrespectful behavior, but also by the fact that this behavior can ruin the experience for others.

A Sensitive Matter:

When dealing with the unfortunate and frequently traumatic history that is involved with many morbid attractions, sensitivity is very necessary.

It is important for both visitors and those creating content to be conscious of the possible emotional impact that their actions and narratives may have on others.

The act of preserving:

The preservation of things is a very important ethical consideration. Historical places, antiques, and memorials are sometimes a part of macabre tourist destinations. It is of the utmost significance to make certain that these locations are protected for the benefit of future generations.

The Persistent Appeal of Sickly Amusements and Places

Even after undergoing significant change and development over the course of time, morbid attractions have managed to maintain their enduring charm. Individuals continue to be captivated by the human preoccupation with the darker parts of existence. This preoccupation may have its origins in simple curiosities, the significance of historical and cultural events, emotional relevance, education and enlightenment, novel experiences, or the impact of popular culture.

The pervasive interest in the macabre that exists within human civilization can be seen reflected in the development and progression of ghastly attractions over time. The concept of morbid attractions has evolved throughout history, from ancient Rome all the way up to the digital age, to accommodate shifting cultural, societal, and technological landscapes. The fascination that modern audiences have for these attractions stems from their natural curiosities, their significant cultural roles, and their insatiable yearning for one-of-a-kind adventures. As macabre attractions continue to develop and find new ways to express themselves, new understandings are being gained on the intricate relationship that exists between fascination and the more macabre aspects of existence. These new understandings shed light on the ever-present relevance that these activities have in the human experience.

Chapter 3

Modern Morbid Attractions

As a result of evolving cultural landscapes, developing technology capabilities, and shifting societal ideals, morbid attractions have taken on new dimensions in the modern period. These modern expressions of macabre are the result of a complicated interaction between historical legacies, popular culture, and various forms of tourism and entertainment that have developed throughout time. Modern morbid attractions offer a diverse investigation of humanity's persistent obsession with the darkest parts of existence. These include haunted attractions, dark tourism locations, true crime media, and virtual experiences. This study dives into the various incarnations of contemporary morbid attractions, shedding light on the cultural significance of these attractions, as well as the ethical questions they raise and the impact they have on modern society.

The study of places associated with tragedy and suffering is referred to as "dark tourism"

The concept of "dark tourism," which encompasses travels to areas connected with death, calamity, violence, and the macabre, has arisen as a significant component of contemporary "morbid attractions." Visitors can connect with historical narratives, confront hard realities, and reflect on the human experience in the backdrop of tragedy and suffering when they participate in this type of tourism.

Monuments to the Fallen and the Battlefields:

Dark tourism has been increasingly popular in recent years, and one of the most common types of sites for it are battlefields from historical battles such as World War I and World War II. People travel to these areas to pay their respects to the soldiers who died there, to educate themselves on the harsh realities of war, and to develop a better comprehension of the toll that war takes on human lives. The perspectives of both combatants and civilians during times of conflict can be gained through visits to museums and memorials dedicated to the conflict.

Memorials to the Holocaust and Sites of Genocide:

A potent reminder of the horrors committed against oppressed populations can be seen in the form of memorials and museums that are dedicated to events such as the Holocaust and other genocides. Such places as Auschwitz-Birkenau in Poland and the Killing Fields in Cambodia provide sad reflections on the horrors of mass violence and the necessity of remembrance in averting future crimes. These places are located in Poland and Cambodia, respectively.

These websites also act as instructional tools to encourage tolerance and understanding of differing viewpoints and perspectives.

Areas Prone to Catastrophe and Other Tragedies:
Natural and man-made disaster sites, such as Chernobyl in the Ukraine and the 9/11 Memorial in New York City, are popular tourist destinations for people who are interested in learning about the effects of calamities on local communities and the surrounding environment. Dark tourism in these regions provides opportunity for meditation on the precarious nature of life, the consequences of human activities, and the resiliency of populations that have been impacted by disasters.

Paranormal Investigations and Haunted Attractions are Available

As immersive kinds of morbid fascination, haunted attractions and paranormal experiences have gained popularity as a sort of modern entertainment known as the haunted attraction. These attractions offer audiences that are looking for adrenaline-fueled adventures experiences that are exhilarating and spine-chilling by combining theatrical performances, interactive storylines, and aspects of horror.

Theme Parks & Spooky Attractions: Haunted Houses

A simulated experience of coming face to face with ghosts, monsters, and other supernatural creatures can be had by guests of haunted houses and other attractions found in theme parks. These attractions are typically located in frightening settings and feature elaborate sets and special effects. The thrill-seekers and horror fans who are looking for entertainment that will get their adrenaline pumping and the exhilaration of facing the unknown in a safe setting will find what they are looking for at one of these attractions.

Ghost Hunting and Other Forms of Paranormal Research:

Participants in paranormal investigations and ghost tours are given the opportunity to investigate supposedly haunted areas and take part in activities like EVP (Electronic Voice Phenomena) recordings, spirit box sessions, and ghost hunts. These encounters give people the opportunity to dig into the secrets of the supernatural and the inexplicable, which fosters a sense of wonder and curiosity about the afterlife and spiritual phenomena.

The True Crime Genre in the Media and in Stories

The explosion of real crime media in recent years, such as documentaries, podcasts, television shows, and books, has made a substantial contribution to the present morbid fascination with death and gore. These storylines dig into real-life criminal cases, unsolved mysteries, and forensic investigations, and they captivate audiences with their research of the complexities of criminal psychology, law enforcement methods, and the pursuit of justice.

Podcasts and docs on the internet:

Documentaries and podcasts that focus on true crimes provide in-depth analyses of criminal cases, providing profiles of the individuals who committed the crimes, as well as the victims, as well as the complex web of circumstances that surrounded the crimes. These narratives frequently place an emphasis on the resiliency of survivors, the dedication of law enforcement professionals, and the long-lasting impact that terrible acts have on communities and families.

Dramatizations and Other Series Broadcast on Television:

Dramatized depictions of criminal investigations, trials, and the aftermath of prominent crimes are provided to viewers of television programs and dramatizations based on actual crime stories. These films present detailed character depictions and narrative arcs that strive to humanize the persons involved in these instances. As a result, they stimulate conversations about the intricacies of criminal behavior and the societal issues that lead to criminality.

Digital Environments and Alternative Forms of Interaction

The advent of the internet age has made it possible to create virtual experiences and interactive digital platforms, which give consumers the opportunity to interact with macabre attractions without having to leave the comfort of their own homes. Individuals now have the opportunity to explore the macabre through virtual reality simulations, internet forums, and social media groups. These platforms also allow users to share their experiences and participate in debates regarding various aspects of dark tourism and entertainment.

Simulations Done in Virtual Reality:

Users are provided with immersive experiences of exploring haunted locales, historical landmarks, and murder scenes through the use of virtual reality simulations. These simulations provide a sense of presence as well as interactivity, which improves the excitement of engaging with macabre attractions. Individuals are given the opportunity to explore simulated environments, engage in conversations with simulated characters, and solve puzzles while immersed in a simulated environment through the use of these simulations.

Online Discussion Groups and Communities on Social Media:

Dark tourism, haunted sites, and true crime are all topics that have their own online communities and discussion forums, which encourage passionate debate and the exchange of information between fans and subject matter specialists. In order to foster a sense of community and camaraderie among those who have similar interests, the aforementioned platforms function as meeting places where users may talk and share their perspectives on a variety of macabre attractions, as well as share their personal experiences, make recommendations for travel destinations, and discuss various hypotheses.

Ethical Considerations Regarding Today's Disgusting Attractions

Ethical questions have become increasingly significant in conversations surrounding responsible involvement with sensitive topics and historical events as the popularity of modern morbid attractions continues to grow.

Having Respect for the Significance of History:

It is essential that the historical relevance of dark tourism locations, haunted attractions, and true crime narratives be respected in order to ensure that the authenticity of these types of encounters is not compromised. When approaching these topics, visitors and those who create content need to have a profound understanding of the seriousness of the occurrences and the effect they have on the communities and individuals who are engaged.

A Sensitive Approach to Trauma and Loss:

It is necessary for those involved in the creation and consumption of modern morbid attractions to have sensitivity to the experiences of persons who have been affected by tragedy, violence, and loss. It is of the utmost importance to ensure that the dignity of victims and their families is preserved by recognizing the emotional weight of the tales and experiences that have been shared.

Finding a Happy Medium Between Entertainment and Learning:

A vitally important ethical aspect is striking a healthy balance between the teaching potential and the entertainment appeal of macabre attractions. These tourist destinations are not only exciting and entertaining, but they also have the ability to teach visitors about the nuances of criminal conduct, the tenacity of human societies, and the complexities of historical events.

Influence on Culture and Its Repercussions Throughout Society

The modern morbid attractions have left a considerable effect on contemporary culture, reflecting the broader societal interests, ideals, and studies of the human psyche that are taking place. They act as mirrors that reflect the complexity of human nature, the fascination of the unknown, and the never-ending desire for comprehension of the most sinister facets of existence.

Since the dawn of the modern period, tourist destinations that cater to our continuing preoccupation with the macabre have morphed into complex representations of this interest. The modern morbid attractions that have become a part of contemporary culture range from dark tourism destinations that explore sites of tragedy and suffering to haunted attractions that offer immersive experiences, true crime media that investigates the complexities of criminal behavior, and virtual experiences that provide interactive engagement.

The cultural influence of these attractions highlights the relevance of their significance in reflecting social interests and the continual investigation of the human experience, while the ethical considerations that surround these attractions highlight the importance of engaging with delicate topics in a responsible manner. In response to shifting cultural landscapes and advances in technology, morbid attractions continue to develop, and as a result, they offer us a prism through which we can better grasp the nuanced and everlasting interaction that exists between the things that fascinate us and the more disturbing aspects of existence.

3.1 Key dark tourism destinations around the world

Dark tourism, a subgenre of travel that involves going to places linked with death, misery, tragedy, and the macabre, has become increasingly common all around the world. These locations provide tourists with the opportunity to interact with historical tales, face unsettling realities, and reflect on the human experience in the context of tragedy and suffering. This investigation dives into some of the most important dark tourism places on a variety of continents, offering insight on the historical relevance, cultural context, and ethical considerations associated with each one.

Historical Battlefields and Places of Memorialization Across Europe
Located in Poland, the Auschwitz-Birkenau Concentration Camp:
The concentration camp known as Auschwitz-Birkenau is widely regarded as one of the most notorious icons of the Holocaust. People travel to this location to pay their respects to the victims of Nazi atrocities, obtain a deeper appreciation of the human cost of intolerance and prejudice, and learn about the horrors of the Holocaust. The memorials, exhibitions, and buildings that have been preserved at the concentration camp are all potent reminders of the urgent need to put an end to atrocities of this kind in the future.

Exclusion Zone around Chernobyl in Ukraine:
The Chernobyl Exclusion Zone is a chilling reminder of the devastation that may be caused by a nuclear accident. Both the abandoned settlement of Pripyat as well as the Chernobyl nuclear power facility are open to tourists for exploration. The zone offers insights into the immediate aftermath of the Chernobyl tragedy, as well as the long-term influence on the ecosystem and the communities that were impacted by the accident.

Memorial to the Victims of the Srebrenica Genocide, Bosnia and Herzegovina:
The Srebrenica Genocide Memorial was built to honor the victims of the atrocities committed by Bosnian Serb troops during the Bosnian War in 1995. These atrocities resulted in the deaths of thousands of Bosnian Muslims.

Visitors will have the opportunity to educate themselves about the conflict, pay their respects at the memorial, and participate in the ongoing process of commemoration and reconciliation.

A Consideration of the Mass Casualties and the Cultural Significance of Asia
Memorial to the Sacrifice of Peace at Hiroshima, Japan:
The Hiroshima Peace Memorial, commonly referred to as the Atomic Bomb Dome, is a sobering reminder of the city of Hiroshima being destroyed by an atomic bomb during World War II. Visitors have the opportunity to tour the Hiroshima Peace Memorial Park while at the site, which serves as a symbol of peace and anti-nuclear

sentiment. The park features museums and monuments that are dedicated to the memory of the victims.

Cambodia's Killing Fields, an Overview:

The Killing Fields are a set of places in Cambodia that were used during the late 1970s by the Khmer Rouge dictatorship for the purpose of carrying out mass executions as well as mass burials. Visitors have the opportunity to pay their respects to the victims of the Cambodian genocide while also learning about the history of the Khmer Rouge and the genocide that occurred in Cambodia. As a component of the Killing Fields, the Choeung Ek Genocidal Center features a memorial stupa that is adorned with the skeletons of those who perished there.

The Temple of the Golden Sun in India:

One of the most sacred places in Sikhism is located in Amritsar, India, and it is known as the Golden Temple. The Akal Takht, which is located within the temple complex, has been a witness to many sad occurrences throughout the history of the Sikh religion. Visitors get the opportunity to gain knowledge about not just the Sikh religion and its history, but also the difficulties and struggles that the Sikh community has endured.

Sites in North America That Inspire National Mourning and Introspection

The United States' National 9/11 Memorial and Museum:

The memorial and museum dedicated to the victims of the terrorist events that occurred on September 11, 2001, can be found in New York City. Visitors have the opportunity to pay their respects to those who lost their lives, gain knowledge about the events that transpired on that tragic day, and interact with narratives that highlight resiliency and unity. The museum features relics, exhibits, and personal accounts that together offer visitors with a holistic perspective of the attacks and the effects they had.

Island of Alcatraz, located in the United States:

"The Rock," also known as Alcatraz Island, is famous for having been the location of a notorious federal prison in the past. Visitors have the opportunity to learn about the history of the jail, its most infamous inmates, and the problems that were experienced by both the prisoners and the guards. In addition, Alcatraz provides breathtaking vistas of San Francisco Bay.

Located in the United States, the National Civil Rights Museum:

Martin Luther King Jr., a prominent figure in the civil rights movement, was killed in Memphis, Tennessee, in 1968, and the location of his funeral is now home to the National Civil Rights Museum. The museum investigates the history of the civil rights movement in the United States, the fight for equality, and the legacy left by the work of Dr. King. It is intended to be a place for contemplation and the dissemination of information regarding the struggle for civil rights.

Commemorating Africa's Struggles and Independence from Colonial Rule
Robben Island, in the Republic of South Africa:

Robben Island is most well-known for its use as a political jail during the time of apartheid in South Africa. The island can be found just off the coast of Cape Town. Visitors can enjoy guided tours of the former jail, which once housed famous political personalities such as Nelson Mandela while he was serving his sentence. The struggle against racial discrimination and the path to liberation are both represented by the island, which acts as a symbol for both.

Memorial to the Victims of the Genocide in Kigali, Rwanda:

The Kigali Genocide Memorial is a melancholy place that was built to remember the genocide that occurred in Rwanda in 1994. Visitors will be able to gain an understanding of the chain of events that led up to the genocide, its catastrophic effects, and Rwanda's efforts toward healing and peace since the genocide. Exhibits, a cemetery, and a garden dedicated to remembering those who have passed are all part of the memorial.

Testimony to the Existence of Political Conflicts in South America

The Chilean Museum of Memory and Human Rights:

The memory of individuals who suffered under the military dictatorship led by Augusto Pinochet is honored at the Museum of Memory and Human Rights in Santiago, Chile. This museum is located in the Chilean capital city. Exhibits are available for guests to examine that provide documentation of violations of human rights, the perspectives of those who have been victimized, and the ongoing search for justice and accountability.

Memorial to the Battle of the Malvinas, Argentina:

The Malvinas War Memorial is located in Buenos Aires, Argentina, and serves as a memorial to the conflict that occurred between Argentina and the United Kingdom during the Falklands War in 1982. In addition to commemorating the service members who were killed in action during the war, the location offers visitors a chance to ponder the repercussions of combat.

The Cultural and Historical Significance of Oceania's Indigenous Heritage

Located in Australia, the Port Arthur Historic Site:

During the 19th century, those convicted of crimes were transported to Port Arthur Historic Site in Tasmania, which was formerly a prison colony. Visitors have the opportunity to visit ancient structures that have been meticulously conserved, acquire knowledge about the severe conditions of penal colonies in Australia, and learn about the life of convicts.

Pearl Harbor in Hawaii, United States of America:

The infamous attack on Pearl Harbor, which was carried out by Japanese forces on the island of Oahu in Hawaii on December 7, 1941, was the event that prompted the United States to get involved in World War II. Visitors get the opportunity to view the USS Arizona Memorial as well as other historical monuments that pay tribute to those who were killed in the attack.

A Look at Some Ethical Aspects of the Dark Tourism Industry

Honoring the Memories of Those Who Have Passed:
When visiting these locations, showing respect for the victims' memories is of the utmost importance. Visitors to these locations must to approach them with delicacy and regard, avoiding behavior that could be construed as disrespectful to the people who have passed away or to the significance of the area.

Value and sensitivity in terms of education:
It is essential to strike a balance between the educational value of these locations and the requirement for sensitivity. It is essential to make people aware of the historical events that took place and the repercussions of those events, while also recognizing the emotional weight that these events entail.

The act of preserving and maintaining:
The protection and upkeep of these historic locations are absolutely necessary in order to guarantee that future generations will be able to benefit from them. The authenticity of these locations can be preserved via appropriate care and conservation efforts.

Making a Difference in the Communities Around Us:
Visitors should engage in dark tourism in a way that shows respect for the local culture and is beneficial to the community if they want to make a positive contribution to local economies and communities.

Dark tourism destinations may be found all over the world and give visitors a wide variety of unique experiences. These might range from memorials and historical battlegrounds to places of cultural value and quiet introspection. When people visit these locations, they help to perpetuate the memory of victims, advance education, and contribute to a deeper comprehension of the intricacies that have characterized human history. Ethical concerns should drive ethical contact with historical sites in order to preserve the respect that should be accorded to the past. Dark tourism offers a one-of-a-kind and potent approach to confronting the darker parts of human existence, reflecting on sorrow and tragedy, and gaining insight from the lessons that history has to teach.

3.2 Famous sites, such as Auschwitz, Chernobyl, and Alcatraz

In recent years, there has been a rise in the phenomenon known as "dark tourism," which refers to the practice of traveling to locations linked with death, pain, tragedy, and the macabre. It provides visitors with the opportunity to connect with historical narratives, confront hard realities, and reflect on the human experience within the context of tragedy and suffering. A special position is reserved for Auschwitz, Chernobyl, and Alcatraz on the list of the most well-known destinations in the world for "dark tourism." These locations are essential case studies for comprehending the complicated dynamics of dark tourism because of the historical relevance, cultural resonance, and ethical considerations that make them.

The Auschwitz Memorial and Museum: A Solemn Memorial to the Holocaust Importance in the Course of History

The term "Holocaust" is almost always used interchangeably with "Auschwitz," which is located in what is now Poland. The Holocaust was a systematic slaughter carried out by Nazi Germany during World War II. It is composed of a number of concentration and extermination camps, the most infamous of which being Auschwitz I and Auschwitz II-Birkenau. Auschwitz I was the first camp, while Birkenau was the extermination camp.

Over one million innocent people, predominantly Jews, but also Roma, political prisoners, and others, were subjected to harsh conditions, forced labor, and mass murder at the Auschwitz concentration camp. As a result, Auschwitz has a somber position in the annals of history. The complex came to represent the barbarism and bigotry of the Nazi regime as well as the worst period in the annals of contemporary history.

Experience of the Visitor:

The former concentration camp of Auschwitz is now a museum and memorial that honors the victims of the Holocaust and encourages people to learn more about what happened there. Visitors have the opportunity to see the barracks, gas chambers, and crematoria that have been maintained. Here, the atrocities of the past are brought to life through exhibitions, artifacts, and human testimonials. The guided tours provide guests a somber and instructive experience, immersing them in the history of the camp as well as the experiences of the people who were incarcerated there.

Considerations of an Ethical Nature:

Visiting Auschwitz is fraught with moral dilemmas and should be done with caution. The utmost importance is placed on showing attention to the historical setting and respect for the victims' memories. Visitors are required to approach the place with reverence and refrain from engaging in any behavior that can be deemed disrespectful to the memory of the departed. It is important that the educational value of Auschwitz be weighed against the requirement for sensitivity, and that the emotional weight of the narratives it holds be acknowledged.

Influence on Culture and the World:

The legacy that Auschwitz has left in terms of culture and the world at large is incalculable. It is a worldwide symbol of the Holocaust and a reminder to remember the tragedies of the past in order to prevent a repeat of such atrocities in the future. Understanding, tolerance, and memory are all promoted through the use of the site, making it an essential component of Holocaust teaching. A further lesson to be learned from Auschwitz is the strength of the human spirit, as well as the importance of seeking justice and being accountable for one's actions.

Investigating the Repercussions of the Nuclear Accident at Chernobyl
Importance in the Course of History:

The Chernobyl Exclusion Zone is located in Ukraine and contains the site of the Chernobyl nuclear disaster, which is considered to be one of the worst nuclear mishaps in the history of the planet. The Chernobyl Nuclear Power Plant experienced a catastrophic explosion in 1986, which resulted in the release of huge amounts of radioactive material into the atmosphere, which in turn resulted in widespread pollution and negative health implications.

The nuclear power plant tragedy at Chernobyl is historically noteworthy because it serves as a vivid reminder of the perils of nuclear power, the repercussions of a technological failure, and the resilience of people that were impacted by the disaster.

Experience of the Visitor:

Visitors visiting Chernobyl have the opportunity to see the deserted city of Pripyat, which consists of settlements that were once vibrant but now stand frozen in time. The immediate aftermath of the tragedy, the emergency response, and the ongoing attempts to manage the radioactive contamination are discussed in detail during guided tours that are available.

The actual Chernobyl Nuclear Power Plant is part of the site, and visitors will have the opportunity to look inside the sarcophagus that encases the malfunctioning reactor. Exploring the aftermath of the Chernobyl tragedy offers a one-of-a-kind opportunity, albeit a spooky one, for visitors to the Chernobyl Exclusion Zone.

Considerations of an Ethical Nature:

At Chernobyl, ethical concerns center on protecting people and participating in activities in a responsible manner. Visitors are obligated to comply with stringent restrictions and show due regard for the established safety regulations. There is also the moral obligation to reflect on and gain wisdom from the Chernobyl catastrophe, which serves as a forceful reminder of the myriad of negative outcomes that could result from the use of nuclear power.

Influence on Culture and the World:

The cultural and worldwide influence of the Chernobyl disaster extends beyond the realm of nuclear safety. It brings to light the precarious nature of human-made systems, the repercussions on the natural world, as well as the aftereffects of a catastrophic event throughout time. The location is used as a teaching tool to illustrate the importance of transparency in the nuclear sector as well as risk management.

The Notorious Prison on the Island of Alcatraz

Importance in the Course of History:

It is well known that the island of Alcatraz in San Francisco Bay served as the location of a notorious federal prison that was in operation from 1934 to 1963. As a result of housing some of history's most notorious felons, such as Al Capone and Robert Stroud, the prison on the island has a reputation for being nearly impossible to break out of.

The segregation of high-profile and potentially dangerous inmates at Alcatraz stands out as a significant event in the history of the American criminal justice system. The enormous expenditures of maintaining the jail and worries about its capacity to rehabilitate offenders led to the institution's decision to close its doors.

Experience of the Visitor:

DEATHLY DELIGHTS

Today, Alcatraz Island serves as a renowned tourist destination that provides visitors with the opportunity to take part in guided tours of the prison's facilities. Visitors are welcome to examine the cells, hallways, and learn about the facility's past. The history of the former prison has been maintained, and informative displays offer visitors a look into the daily routines of both the prisoners and the guards who worked there.

Considerations of an Ethical Nature:

At Alcatraz, ethical concerns center on how the institution's past should be presented in a responsible manner. The history of the island includes the cruel treatment of prisoners, the maintenance of difficult conditions, and the occurrence of infrequent acts of savagery. The site requires both visitors and curators to treat it with sensitivity and a dedication to providing a narrative that is balanced and accurate about its history.

Influence on Culture and the World:

The importance of Alcatraz in popular culture in the United States is directly related to its cultural and global effect. It has been featured in a large number of movies and television series, which has contributed to the solidification of its notoriety. The American Indian takeover of Alcatraz, which took place from 1969 to 1971 and is considered a watershed moment in the history of Native American civil rights, took place on the island as well.

An Examination of Comparative Cases: Alcatraz, Auschwitz, and Chernobyl

Importance in the Course of History:

The historical relevance of Auschwitz, Chernobyl, and Alcatraz is entirely distinct from one another. The concentration camp known as Auschwitz is well recognized as a symbol of the Holocaust. This image conveys the unspeakable horrors of genocide as well as the atrocities committed by the Nazi dictatorship. It is important to remember the lessons that can be learned from the Chernobyl nuclear tragedy and other examples of technological failure. In contrast, Alcatraz provides a living example of the difficulties associated with high-security confinement in the middle of the 20th century as well as the representation of criminality in popular culture.

Experience of the Visitor:

The experiences that visitors get at each of these locations are very different from one another. The experience at Auschwitz is one that is both mournful and informative, with a focus on remembering the past and teaching about the Holocaust. The aftermath of the Chernobyl tragedy may be experienced in an unsettling and fully immersive manner at Alcatraz, in contrast to the prison facilities at Chernobyl, which can be toured by tourists at Alcatraz.

Considerations of an Ethical Nature:

These websites do not function without taking ethical considerations into account. Because of its relationship with the Holocaust, visiting Auschwitz calls for the highest level of respect and understanding. Because of Chernobyl, we have a responsibility to work with radioactive leftovers in a safe and responsible manner. The presentation of the tale of Alcatraz must be fair and take into account the severe conditions of the jail as well as its long history of cruel treatment.

Influence on Culture and the World:

The places have a significant impact both on culture and on the global community. It is important to remember the Holocaust and educate future generations about it, and Auschwitz plays a significant role in both of these endeavors. The disaster at Chernobyl draws attention to the dangers posed by nuclear technology and the adverse effects on the environment. In addition to being an iconic figure in popular culture, Alcatraz has come to represent a certain type of high-security confinement in the United States and has been linked to many Native American civil rights campaigns.

Examples of the diversity that may be found among dark tourist locations include Auschwitz, Chernobyl, and Alcatraz. They are emblems that represent the relevance of history, the resonance of culture, and the complexities of ethics. The narratives of tragedy, sorrow, and resilience that are shared at these locations provide visitors with an opportunity to reflect on the more negative aspects of human existence. These travel places have an influence that is felt well beyond their geographic locations, contributing to a better global understanding as well as cultural representations and societal lessons. Each in its own way, Auschwitz, Chernobyl, and Alcatraz compels us to reflect on the past, gain knowledge from it, and face it head-on while also considering the present and the future.

3.3 Emerging trends and destinations in dark tourism

Over the course of the last few decades, there has been a notable expansion in the phenomenon known as "dark tourism," which refers to the habit of traveling to locations linked with death, pain, tragedy, and the macabre. Dark tourism has become increasingly popular as an increasing number of individuals look for travel experiences that are not only one of a kind but also provoke deep reflection. This pattern has resulted in the introduction of new destinations as well as shifts in the expectations that visitors have.

In the course of this investigation, we will look into the developing patterns and locations in dark tourism, as well as the elements that are contributing to the industry's ongoing evolution.

The first trend is customized and all-encompassing experiences.

The demand for individualized and all-encompassing experiences has emerged as one of the most important tendencies in the field of dark tourism. Passive observation is no longer sufficient for visitors; instead, they want to actively participate with the tales and locations that they are viewing. As a response, travel companies and locations are beginning to provide visitors with more engaging and immersive experiences. Some examples of these include guided reenactments, escape rooms, and interactive displays. Visitors visiting the Auschwitz-Birkenau Concentration Camp, for instance, have the opportunity to take part in guided tours that imitate the experiences of prisoners. As a result, they gain a deeper comprehension of the agony that was endured during the Holocaust.

The second trend is the enhancement of digital and augmented reality.

The development of new technologies has been an essential factor in determining the course that dark tourism will take in the years to come. Experiences that combine elements of augmented reality (AR) and virtual reality (VR) are becoming more widespread. These experiences enable visitors to explore historical locations and interact with narratives in a manner that is both more participatory and educational. For example, the Chernobyl Exclusion Zone has begun giving virtual reality (VR) tours that allow visitors to undertake an interactive journey of the abandoned city of Pripyat and provide a look into life prior to the nuclear tragedy.

Off-the-beaten-path destinations are the subject of the third trend.

There is a growing interest in going to places that are off the beaten path because many of the most popular areas for dark tourism are being overrun with visitors. Travelers are looking for lesser-known destinations that tell equally captivating stories. This trend is a reflection of people's desire for experiences that are less commercialized and more genuine. For instance, the S-21 Prison in Phnom Penh, Cambodia, which was utilized by the Khmer Rouge administration, has received interest as an alternative to more visited dark tourism attractions. This prison is located in the same city as the Killing Fields.

The Fourth Tendency: Conservation and Reconstruction

To protect the historical significance of a great number of dark tourism destinations, preservation and restoration work is currently in progress. There is an increasing awareness among governments and groups of the significance of preserving these locations for future generations. Such efforts include, for instance, the ongoing restoration of the sites in South Africa associated with the Soweto Uprising. These locations, which were once the scene of rallies against apartheid, are being maintained so that future tourists can learn about the fight for freedom and equality.

Tend 5 : Tourism with a Particular Focus on the Dark

The investigation of particular topics within the realm of dark tourism is becoming an increasingly popular trend. These topics may include the history of medicine, crimes, or natural disasters. Within the more general realm of dark tourism, these topics make it possible to delve more deeply into specific subcultures' interests. For instance, the Mutter Museum in Philadelphia draws tourists who are interested in the macabre aspects of the medical industry since it is famous for its collection of antique medical tools and unusual artifacts related to medicine.

Emerging Markets for the Nighttime Tourism Industry

The Site of the Massacre at Wounded Knee, in the United States:

People who are interested in Native American history and the events that surrounded the killing of Lakota Sioux people in 1890 should consider visiting the Wounded Knee killing Site in South Dakota. The site has earned prominence as a destination for those with such interests. Visitors will be able to gain an understanding of the challenges faced by native communities as well as the importance of this historical location.

Dark Sky Parks in a Number of Different Locations:
Stargazers and anyone interested in astronomy are driving the increase in popularity of dark sky parks. These approved sites have low levels of light pollution, making them fantastic places to go stargazing and observe the night sky. Some of these parks provide their guests with educational opportunities and guided excursions, allowing them to investigate the unfathomable mysteries of the cosmos.

The Devastation of Detroit, in the United States:
Because of its many vacant homes, factories, and other buildings, the city of Detroit in the state of Michigan is becoming a popular destination for "dark tourism." These ruins serve as a canvas for urban exploration and photography in addition to providing a view into the city's economic downfall and urban degradation.

Sites of Reconciliation, Located in Various Places:
People who are interested in social justice and reconciliation are increasingly likely to travel to sites of reconciliation, which are gathering places where past conflicts and injustices are acknowledged. Some examples are the sites that were created by the Truth and Reconciliation Commission in South Africa. These sites focus on the transition from apartheid to reconciliation in the country.

The Contributing Factors to the Development of Dark Tourism

The media and the culture of pop:
The depiction of dark tourist destinations in movies, television shows, and documentaries has piqued audiences' interest and piqued their appetite for knowledge. The media has the ability to bring less well-known locations to the public's attention and raise awareness of the practice.

Shifting Priorities and Consciousness:
The increase in the popularity of dark tourism can be attributed, in part, to societal movements toward increased empathy, understanding of human rights, and a desire for education. A growing number of people are interested in gaining a knowledge of historical atrocities and catastrophes.

Recent Developments in Technology:
The incorporation of technology, such as augmented reality (AR), virtual reality (VR), and digital storytelling, is improving the experience that visitors have. Through the use of technology, visitors to dark tourism destinations can have more engaging and informative experiences.

Conservation of Cultural Property:
As the historical significance of dark tourism sites becomes more widely acknowledged, preservation initiatives are being undertaken, and access for tourists is being expanded. There is a concerted effort being made by many governments and groups to preserve and safeguard these locations for future generations.

Tour Operators Specializing in Their Field:
Tour companies that focus on dark tourism typically provide customers with a diverse selection of activities and itineraries to choose from. These knowledgeable individuals are responsible for the organization of dark tourism itineraries that cover a wide range of topics, from the history of violent conflicts to accounts of criminal activities.

A Look at Some Ethical Aspects of the Dark Tourism Industry
Regard for the Lives Lost and Those That Survived:
The memories of those who were killed at dark tourism locations should be treated with care, and visitors should be sensitive to the experiences of those who survived. It is important to prevent behavior that is disrespectful as well as sensationalism.

Finding a Middle Ground Between Education and Sensitivity:
Even while black tourism has educational value, operators need to be mindful of the psychological toll it takes on tourists. The sites have a responsibility to find a middle ground between telling historical narratives and recognizing the emotional gravity of the stories they tell.

A Respect for Culture:
Visitors are expected to show respect for the local cultures and communities that surround locations of dark tourism. The financial benefits of tourism shouldn't come at the expense of the cultural value and the dignity of the locations that are being visited.

Authenticity and openness to the public:
Both tour operators and locations have a responsibility to give information that is truthful and open. When it comes to maintaining the credibility of dark tourism experiences, authenticity is absolutely necessary.

The constantly shifting terrain of dark tourism is a monument to the human quest for insight and introspection. The need for more personalized and immersive experiences, which is being driven by advances in technology as well as a greater engagement with historical tales, is reflected in newly emerging trends. When previously unknown places are discovered, new insights into human history, as well as its tragedies and triumphs, can be gained from visiting them. Ethical considerations continue to drive appropriate engagement with dark tourism, ensuring that the memory of victims and the value of the places are respected throughout the process. Dark tourism provides tourists with a one-of-a-kind and potent method for tackling the more negative parts of human existence. It gives guests the opportunity to recall, learn about, and reflect on the past while simultaneously looking to the future.

Chapter 4

The Ethical Dilemmas of Dark Tourism

The concept of "dark tourism," which refers to the act of traveling to locations linked with death, misery, tragedy, and the macabre, has been the topic of heated controversy for a very long time. In spite of the fact that it presents educational, reflective, and remembering opportunities, it also poses difficult moral conundrums. Questions of respect, authenticity, commercialization, and the influence on local communities come to the forefront when visitors engage with sensitive and often horrific history. These questions come to the forefront as visitors engage with these histories. The purpose of this investigation is to shed light on the issues that are experienced by visitors, tour operators, local communities, and the sites themselves. The investigation dives into the various ethical dilemmas that are associated with black tourism.

1. **The Morality of Showing Respect and Being Sensitive**
   Within the realm of dark tourism, two of the most essential ethical considerations are respect for the memories of victims and sensitivity to the experiences of survivors. Visitors are expected to approach these sites with a profound sense of reverence and an awareness of the human suffering and tragedy that these locations symbolize as they travel through them. It is extremely rude and unacceptable to engage in behaviors that make light of or exaggerate the significance of past events. It is essential, in order to treat the sites with the dignity they deserve, to strike a balance between the educational value of the visit and the emotional sensitivity of the experience.
   When visiting Auschwitz-Birkenau, for example, guests are reminded to keep a respectful approach and refrain from engaging in any activity that could be construed as lessening the significance of the Holocaust. Visitors are also asked to dress appropriately. To do this, you must refrain from acting in a manner that displays contempt for the victims and survivors, such as taking pictures, speaking loudly, or taking other similar actions. Similarly, visitors to the Hiroshima

Peace Memorial are encouraged to approach the site with a profound sense of empathy and an awareness of the tragic consequences of the atomic bomb. This is because the memorial was built to commemorate the victims of the bombing of Hiroshima.

2. **Finding a Balance Between Trauma and Education**
When it comes to issues of ethics, one of the most pressing concerns in the field of dark tourism is the delicate balancing act that must be performed between the provision of educational value and the infliction of emotional anguish. Although these sites are extremely useful instructional tools, they also have the potential to cause traumatic reactions in certain visitors, particularly those who had direct personal involvement in the events that took place or who belonged to communities that were adversely affected. A delicate balance that calls for the careful curation of narratives and experiences is required in order to provide authentic historical knowledge without sensationalizing or exploiting the suffering that occurred in the past.

In places like the Killing Fields in Cambodia, where the Khmer Rouge regime was responsible for mass crimes, the problem comes in conveying the historical context and the accounts of survivors in a way that is informative without causing any undue trauma. This is a challenge that is unique to destinations like the Killing Fields. Visitors who find the event emotionally overwhelming may benefit from support and guidance from tour operators and guides who have received training to handle sensitive topics and offer assistance.

3. **The importance of Authenticity in Relation to Commercialization**
The commodification of tourist destinations previously associated with criminal activity raises substantial ethical concerns. As these websites grow in popularity, there is a possibility that they could be transformed into commercial enterprises. This could result in the exploitation of tragic events for the purpose of making a profit. This can lead to the trivialization of historical events and the selling of human pain, both of which weaken the experience's integrity and authenticity. One possible outcome of this is that historical events become less significant.

It is a continuing challenge in places like the 9/11 Memorial and Museum in New York City to maintain a relevant educational experience while avoiding the commercialization of the disaster. This is a task that must be managed in order to find a balance between the two. The method taken by the museum to keep the environment dignified and courteous while also ensuring that it is accessible to tourists underscores the constant ethical issues that are involved in preserving a site of such significance.

4. **Maintaining One's Sense of Dignity While Being Culturally Sensitive**
There are key ethical imperatives that must be met, including as ensuring that the departed are treated with respect and that the cultural sensitivities of the communities that are affiliated with dark tourism sites be honored. Both visitors

and managers of the sites have a responsibility to be aware of the historical and cultural significance of the locations, making certain that the narratives are conveyed in a way that is respectful of the values, customs, and traditions of the people that are impacted.

When it comes to the situation of Robben Island in South Africa, which was used to hold political prisoners during the apartheid era, the ethical problem lies in presenting the experiences of the detainees and their struggles within the larger context of the history of the country. It is also necessary, in order to preserve the authenticity of the event, to show respect for the cultural significance of the location as well as the personal stories of the people who were engaged.

5. **Influence on the Communities in the Area and the Commemoration of It**
A key area of ethical concern is the effect that dark tourism has on the communities that are visited. Tourism has the potential to offer economic benefits to communities; but, it also has the potential to disturb the environment, culture, and the process of remembering in those places. To strike the right balance between managing the influx of tourists and safeguarding the well-being and autonomy of local communities, stakeholders, including local authorities, tour operators, and community leaders, need to work together.

It is essential to practice responsible tourism in areas such as the Srebrenica Genocide Memorial in Bosnia and Herzegovina, where the local population is still working through the effects of the genocide. This type of tourism helps the local economy without interfering with the healing process. This entails the implementation of programs that offer the local community chances for economic growth without capitalizing on the tragedy for financial gain.

6. **Impact of Tourism on the Environment and Sustainable Travel**
Ethical issues of the utmost importance include the propagation of environmentally friendly tourism practices and the analysis of how dark tourism destinations affect the surrounding ecosystem. Due to the legacy of the tragedies that they symbolize, certain locations, such as the Chernobyl Exclusion Zone, have considerable difficulties in terms of their impact on the ecosystem. It is vital, for the long-term viability of these areas, to make certain that the activities associated with tourism do not accelerate the degradation of the environment or pose any threats to the health of visitors.

Managing the environmental impact of tourism operations in the Chernobyl Exclusion Zone while conserving the integrity of the site as a historical witness to the consequences of a nuclear tragedy presents a challenging ethical conundrum. It is essential, in order to ensure the continued profitability of the site, to strike a balance between the requirements of regulated access and the safeguarding of the surrounding environment.

7. **Community Empowerment and the Promotion of Responsible Tourism**

In the context of dark tourism, it is an ethical necessity to encourage practices of responsible tourism that aim to strengthen local communities and make a positive contribution to the wellbeing of such communities. It is vital to engage in activities that preserve the cultural integrity of the communities, support local businesses, and contribute to the preservation of heritage in order to mitigate the negative impact of tourism and develop a relationship between tourists and local inhabitants that is mutually beneficial to both parties.

The Hiroshima Peace Memorial is an example of a destination that exemplifies responsible tourism practices by placing a priority on the engagement and empowerment of the local community. The significance of the memorial may be maintained while also helping the economy of the surrounding area through the implementation of programs that encourage the teaching of peace and involve members of the local community in the administration of the site.

The moral conundrums presented by dark tourism highlight the significance of responsible participation, cultural sensitivity, and a profound comprehension of the impact that these locations have, not just on tourists but also on the communities that surround them. As the concept of "dark tourism" continues to develop, the various parties involved have a responsibility to give high priority to the protection of dignity, the development of sustainable practices, and the empowerment of communities that are directly impacted. Dark tourism has the potential to serve as a method of fostering recollection, education, and reflection, while simultaneously honoring the dignity of the past and contributing to a more compassionate and understanding future. This potential can be realized by navigating these ethical problems with care and sensitivity.

4.1 Ethical concerns and debates surrounding morbid attractions

Since its inception, discussions over the morality of 'morbid attractions,' which are defined as "leisure activities and entertainment that focus on death, suffering, and the macabre," have been ongoing. Although they provide visitors with a one-of-a-kind experience that is frequently educative, they also present a number of difficult ethical problems concerning respect for the people who have passed away, the emotional impact that they have on visitors, the line that separates attraction from exploitation, and the possible desensitization to acts of murder and suffering. During this in-depth investigation, we will delve into the various ethical difficulties and arguments that surround morbid attractions. Our goal is to shed light on the challenges that are encountered by visitors, organizers, and society as a whole.

1. **The Morality of Showing Respect and Being Sensitive**

    The question of respect for the people who have passed away and sensitivity to the suffering of those who were involved is one of the most fundamental ethical concerns that arise in connection with morbid attractions. Visitors are expected to approach all of these events with a tremendous sense of reverence, whether they are going to visit sites of tragedy, reading true crime novels, or taking part in immersive horror experiences.

When paying respects to the departed at cemeteries, burial sites, or mass graves, there is a fine line to walk between showing respect and avoiding any action that could make their memory seem insignificant. Finding this balance can be challenging. Visitors are expected to show respect for the final resting places of the deceased and refrain from engaging in actions that take away from the solemnity of the location when they go to prominent cemeteries such as Père Lachaise in Paris. This cemetery is home to the remains of a large number of historical people.

2. **The Effect on One's Emotional and Mental Health**

The possible psychological effect that this could have on guests is a major source of ethical concern. The sheer nature of morbid attractions means that they frequently expose visitors to stuff that can be upsetting or unsettling for them. Although some guests could be looking for an emotional experience, others might not be ready for the psychological and emotional toll that it might take on them.

For instance, the goals of immersive horror experiences like haunted houses and other severe horror attractions are to cause the participants to feel frightened and uncomfortable. However, event organizers have a responsibility to provide careful consideration to the participants' mental health, given that visitors knowingly put themselves through these experiences for the sake of the excitement. Many ethical discussions center on the question of whether or not individuals are able to give their informed consent to such experiences, as well as the question of whether or not there should be age restrictions or psychological evaluations in place to protect those who may be more susceptible to emotional distress.

3. **The Thin Line That Separates Exploitation from Fascination**

Sometimes the line between fascinating and exploitative is blurred when it comes to morbid attractions. There is a possibility that these attractions may exploit the pain of others for the purpose of amusement or financial gain. Despite the fact that these attractions provide a space for investigation and meditation on the darker parts of existence, there is a danger that they may do so. To discern between respectful fascination and destructive exploitation presents a difficult problem from an ethical standpoint.

Concerns concerning sensationalism and the possible glorification of violent behavior are frequently raised in the context of true crime media when it comes to the representation of criminals and the crimes they engage in. It might be morally questionable to portray horrible acts in a manner that gives the impression of lionizing or romanticizing the individuals who committed the crimes. The argument extends to the responsibilities of media providers and consumers in striking a balance between voyeurism that is not motivated by genuine interest and voyeurism that is motivated by genuine curiosity.

4. **Desensitization to Both Suffering and Physical Conflict**
   Another issue that raises ethical concerns with morbid attractions is the possibility that visitors could become desensitized to acts of cruelty and misery. Individuals might become desensitized to the actual violence and suffering that exists in the world as a result of excessive exposure to gory or upsetting information, which can lead to a numbing effect.
   In the context of violent video games, horror films, and severe terror experiences, ethical discussions frequently center on the question of whether or not there is a connection between the consumption of such media and desensitization to violent behavior. The research on this subject is inconclusive, with some studies finding a link between violent media and increased aggression and others arguing that consumption of media is not a direct cause of violence in the real world.
5. **Commercialization and the Drive to Make a Profit**
   The commodity of death and suffering generates ethical problems that are brought up by the commercialization of morbid attractions. There is a danger, if these attractions continue to grow in popularity, that profit objectives will take precedence over ethical issues. When sorrow and pain are turned into a commodity for financial gain, the authenticity of the event can be compromised, and sensitive stories can be turned into money-making enterprises.
   In the context of ghost tours in historical locations that are known for paranormal activity, the ethical problem lies in striking a balance between offering an entertaining and educational experience for guests and avoiding the overcommercialization of the supernatural. This is a hurdle that must be overcome in order to meet the standards of good business practice. It is possible that some operators will embellish their claims or sensationalize their experiences in order to draw in a greater number of customers. This could potentially rise to ethical questions regarding the operators' honesty and authenticity.
6. **The Importance of Giving Properly Informed Consent**
   A significant number of macabre attractions place an emphasis on the significance of providing visitors with the opportunity to give their informed consent. It is an ethical obligation to ensure that visitors have a complete understanding of what they are consenting to when they knowingly engage with potentially upsetting or frightening information. Visitors may opt to voluntarily engage with such content.
   For instance, participants in extreme horror experiences may knowingly put themselves in situations where they are subjected to simulated acts of violence, gore, and psychological pain. The ability of individuals to give their informed permission for experiences that have the potential to push the boundaries of their emotional and psychological distress is a contentious issue in the realm of ethics. Others contend that participants should take personal responsibility for their decisions and that these attractions should provide exhaustive information

regarding the nature of the content as well as the possible effects it may have on attendees, while others support the former position.

7. **The Effect It Has On Ethics And Values**

   Because morbid attractions have the capacity to change people's views and behaviors, there are ethical concerns regarding the potential for these attractions to have an effect on individuals' morality and values. Exposure to violent content, such as that found in true crime media and violent video games, may influence how individuals perceive and react to violent situations in the real world. This is a particularly important consideration in the case of true crime media and violent video games.

   The duty of media creators and the potential impact of their content on consumers is a topic that is frequently at the heart of the discussion. Others highlight the significance of individual autonomy and the requirement for critical media literacy, while others argue that the media ought to be regulated in order to limit the potential harm that it may cause.

8. **sensitivity to cultural and historical contexts**

   In the field of morbid attractions, preserving cultural and historical sensitivity is a vitally important ethical concern. It is common for the histories and cultures of communities to be intricately linked with the locations of narratives and sites associated with death and suffering. Both visitors and event organizers have a responsibility to be aware of the cultural context and sensitivity of the locations they are visiting.

   For instance, in the subject of war tourism, in which tourists explore battlefields and historical conflict zones, there is a difficult balance to be struck between informing tourists about the historical value of these sites and showing respect for the memories of those who perished at these locations. Many times, discussions on ethics center on who is responsible for demonstrating cultural and historical sensitivity on the part of visitors and tour providers.

9. **The Value of Education in Relation to Entertainment**

   An ongoing source of ethical concern is the conflict that arises in the context of morbid attractions between the educational value they provide and the entertaining value they provide. Although the primary purpose of these attractions is frequently to impart knowledge regarding historical occurrences, the plight of humans, and the more negative aspects of being alive, they may also include elements of fun in order to attract and keep the attention of visitors.

   In the context of museums that are devoted to the history of crime and infamous criminals, the major question at issue is whether or not these types of attractions should put an emphasis on educating visitors rather than entertaining them. There are many who believe that the instructional purposes of these museums may be undermined by the presence of interactive displays, immersive experiences, and dramatic storytelling.

10. **Effects on Society Over the Long Term**

Another ethical worry is the effect that morbid inclinations will have on society in the long run. It's possible that being confronted with death, suffering, and gruesome imagery has far-reaching consequences on the values, empathy, and perceptions of violence and tragedy held by a culture. The potential repercussions of normalizing or trivializing morbid content are frequently at the center of the discussion around ethics.

In the context of real crime documentaries and podcasts, ethical problems arise concerning the influence that such content will have in the long run on public views toward deviant behavior. Others believe that the obsession with genuine crimes and criminals may contribute to a society that celebrates or romanticizes criminality, while others stress the value of using these tales to understand the nuances of criminal conduct. One argument suggests that the fascination with real crimes and criminals may contribute to a culture that glorifies or romanticizes criminality.

The ethics of morbid attractions, such as going to a graveyard or participating in an extreme horror encounter, are a subject of intense debate and concern. Visitors, event organizers, and society as a whole have the responsibility of navigating the complications of showing respect for the deceased, understanding the emotional impact of the event, avoiding exploitation, preventing desensitization, and striking a balance between instructional value and entertaining value.

As the number of people visiting macabre attractions continues to rise, those with a stake in the industry have a responsibility to give ethical issues top priority. This will ensure that investigations into death, suffering, and the macabre are carried out with respect, sensitivity, and a profound understanding of the potential repercussions for both individuals and society. We are able to create a balance between education and entertainment, education and fascination, and the investigation of the darker parts of human existence if we address these ethical problems and engage in discussions that are educated and serious.

4.2 The impact of visitor behavior on sensitive sites

The actions of visitors have a significant impact on sensitive sites, which include a wide variety of locales associated with tragedy, historical upheaval, and cultural significance. These locations, which can be anything from memorials and historical landmarks to natural wonders and religious places, typically possess a great deal of significance both emotionally and historically. The effect that the actions of visitors have on these locations is a complicated and multi-faceted problem that includes ethical, cultural, social, environmental, and economic aspects. This investigation dives into the myriad of ways in which visitor behavior can have an impact on sensitive locations, analyzing both the difficulties and the potential benefits involved with successfully managing these affects.

1. **Considerations of an Ethical Nature**
   Memory of the Past and Deference to Those Who Have Passed
   The requirement to show respect for the departed and appreciate the historical memory they represent is one of the most important ethical issues that should be taken into account regarding visitor behavior at sensitive locations. Visitors are expected to behave respectfully and solemnly while they are at locations such as cemeteries, mass graves, and war memorials. Behavior that is disrespectful or disruptive has the potential to be an affront to the memories of those who have suffered or lost their lives.
   For instance, visitors visiting the Auschwitz-Birkenau Concentration Camp in Poland, which serves as a sharp reminder of the Holocaust, are encouraged to behave with the utmost respect and refrain from indulging in inappropriate behaviors such as taking pictures or having loud conversations. This is because the camp serves as a memorial to the victims of the Holocaust. When visitors to a site fail to recognize the value of the location and accord it the respect it warrants, ethical conundrums might result.
   Striking a Balance Between Curiosity and Sensitivity
   It is important for visitors to behave in a way that satisfies their natural interest while also showing respect for the sensitive nature of the site. Visitors to places connected with catastrophes, such as the Hiroshima Peace Memorial in Japan, are expected to approach these locations with a profound sense of empathy and an awareness of the devastation caused by events such as the dropping of an atomic bomb. To provide an educational environment that is conducive to learning while avoiding insensitivity or trivialization presents a difficult problem from an ethical standpoint.

2. **The Affect It Has Emotionally on Guests**
   Visitors typically experience a tremendous range of feelings when they visit sensitive locations. Depending on the characteristics of the location, visitors may experience feelings that vary from sorrow and grief to awe and inspiration. These feelings have an effect on the conduct of visitors, making it very important for site managers to take into account the visitors' subjective experiences in this regard.
   Providing an Opportunity for Self-Reflection
   Visitors are likely to experience a profound range of feelings when they visit memorials to tragic events, such as the one that stands in New York City and honors those who perished on September 11, 2001. At such locations, the type of conduct that is anticipated is one of reflection and contemplation. The managers of the site are responsible for providing visitors with areas in which they can process their feelings and for providing support services to those who may require them.
   Addressing the Possibility of Feeling Overwhelmed Emotionally

When sensitive places are too emotionally overwhelming for visitors, visitor conduct can also become a cause for worry. In order to prevent visitors from experiencing an emotional overload at memorials like the Oklahoma City National Memorial, which is dedicated to the people who died in the explosion in 1995, meticulous administration is required. The question of whether or not there should be standards or restrictions in place to safeguard those who may find the experience emotionally uncomfortable is frequently at the center of disputes pertaining to ethics.

3. **Sensitivity to and comprehension of other cultures**
Many times, the histories and cultures of the populations that are associated with sensitive sites are intricately intertwined with one another. Visitors and their behavior should be culturally aware and respectful of the local beliefs and traditions when they are visiting the place.
Paying Respect to the Traditions and Customs of the Area
Visitors are expected to observe local customs and traditions when visiting religious sites such as the Western Wall in Jerusalem. Displays of affection in public, for example, are seen to be both rude and offensive in some cultures. This is because such behaviors go against local customs. Ethical considerations center on the requirement that tourists educate themselves about the cultural value of the site and conduct themselves in a manner that is consistent with the norms that are held in the community.

4. **The Tourism Industry's Impact on the Economy and Its Future**
Sensitive locations typically draw in a sizeable number of tourists, and the manner in which these people behave can have a sizeable effect on the local economy of the villages that are located nearby. The local ecology, culture, and the process of commemoration can all be negatively impacted by tourism, despite the fact that it may provide economic benefits. For these impacts to be mitigated, sustainable tourism practices are very necessary.
Communities and their respective local economies
The local community in tourist locations like the Srebrenica Genocide Memorial in Bosnia and Herzegovina benefits significantly economically from the presence of tourists. The necessity of engaging in responsible tourism that bolsters the local economy without interfering with the recuperation process for the community is at the center of the ethical debates that take place. A primary concern is striking a healthy balance between the economic benefits of tourism and respect for the memory of those who have passed away.
Protection of the Environment and Cultural Properties
At sensitive areas, one more component of ethical behavior is sensitivity to the surrounding natural environment. Some of these locations, like the exclusion zone around the Chernobyl nuclear power plant, continue to face environmental issues as a result of the tragedies that took place there in the past. Guests are

required to be conscious of the influence they have on the surrounding environment and to adhere to sustainable tourism principles. Ethical considerations include the requirement that access to sensitive natural areas be restricted in order to maintain the sites' intact natural integrity.

5. **Maintaining the authenticity of culture and history**

   It is absolutely necessary, in order to protect the value of sensitive places, to ensure that their cultural and historical authenticity is preserved. The cultural and historical context in which these places are located should be respected by visitors, both in terms of their behavior and the way they interact with the sites.

   Importance from a Cultural and Historical Perspective

   When participating in war tourism, tourists have a responsibility to recognize the historical value of battlegrounds and conflict zones and to show proper respect for the memories of those who were killed there. It is possible for visitors to a site to create ethical conundrums for themselves if they participate in unethical behavior or are unable to comprehend the cultural and historical context of the location.

   Finding a Happy Medium Between Education and Respect

   The issue for sensitive sites that want to teach visitors about historical events and human suffering is to find a balance between the educational goals of the site and respect for the memories of the people who were part in the events. The question of whether the presenting of narratives should place a greater emphasis on teaching or on the preservation of historical and cultural integrity frequently comes up in discussions of ethics.

6. **Authenticity, as well as Responsible Participation**

   When it comes to protecting the cultural and historical significance of sensitive locations, authenticity is absolutely necessary. Visitors to these sites should interact with them in a responsible and genuine manner, avoiding activities that detract from the overall experience.

   Taking Precautions Against Being Taken Too Lightly

   When visiting places like the Anne Frank House in Amsterdam, which is dedicated to preserving the memory of Anne Frank and the Holocaust, it is imperative to avoid trivializing or sensationalizing the subject matter. This is an important ethical problem. It is anticipated of visitors to the site that they will approach it in an authentic manner, recognizing the historical relevance of the experience as well as the authenticity of the site itself.

   Education as well as Genuine Stories and Accounts

   The provision of genuine narratives and genuine educational opportunities is frequently a requirement for responsible involvement with sensitive locations. For instance, at the South African sites that commemorate the fight against apartheid and the Soweto Uprising, it is vitally important to showcase the stories of the individuals who were involved and to ensure that their experiences are authentically conveyed. Authenticity is essential in both of these endeavors.

7. **Regulations and Guidance for the Tourism Industry**

   It is always important to keep in mind the ethical implications of the role that tourism legislation and guidelines play in molding visitor behavior at sensitive sites. It is common practice for governments and managers of these sites to establish regulations and guidelines in order to ensure responsible behavior and preserve the authenticity of these sites.

   Maintaining an Attitude of Respect

   There are restrictions and procedures in place at tourist spots, such as the Pearl Harbor National Memorial in Hawaii, to ensure that tourists conduct themselves in a polite manner. Discussions on ethics center on striking a balance between the right to one's own personal liberty and the obligation to preserve the memory of those who have been killed.

   Protection and Safekeeping

   The protection and well-being of guests should also be considered an ethical priority. Due to the historical significance of the location and the possible emotional impact the location may have on visitors, it is of the utmost importance that tourists be kept safe at places like the Hiroshima Peace Memorial. When trying to strike a balance between allowing tourists access to a place and watching out for their well-being, there are bound to be some difficult moral choices to make.

8. **Raise People's Awareness and Educate Them**

   Education and awareness campaigns have the potential to mold the manner in which visitors behave at sensitive places. The purpose of these projects is to educate visitors about the historical, cultural, and emotional value of the place, as well as to direct them on how to behave appropriately while there.

   Programs for Instructional Purposes

   Educational programs are provided in locations such as the Gettysburg National Military Park in the United States to educate tourists about the historical significance of the location they are visiting, such as the American Civil War. These programs intend to foster behavior that is courteous toward others and an awareness of the importance of the location. Ethical issues emphasize the importance of engaging in all-encompassing educational endeavors.

   Campaigns to Raise Awareness among the Public

   Public awareness campaigns are frequently important contributors to the process of molding visitor behavior. Campaigns, such as those held at the Nagasaki Atomic Bomb Museum in Japan, for instance, aim to increase awareness about the horrors of nuclear weapons and the necessity of maintaining peace. The role of websites to give exhaustive information and to encourage polite behavior is at the heart of the ethical disputes that take place.

9. Repercussions for the Actual Location

The actions of visitors can also have a direct and tangible effect on environmentally sensitive areas. Large numbers of visitors can cause wear and tear, which in turn requires efforts to be made toward maintenance and conservation.

There is the possibility that visitors will accidentally do damage to the site, which poses ethical considerations around the maintenance of the site's physical integrity.

Efforts Made Regarding Conservation

In places like Machu Picchu in Peru, where the historical and cultural significance of the monument must be preserved at all costs, conservation measures are absolutely necessary. Because of the substantial number of visitors, the location must undergo persistent upkeep and conservation efforts in order to be protected for the foreseeable future. Many discussions about ethics center on the question of whether or not there should be visitor quotas and what constitutes sustainable tourism activities.

Considerations relating to ethics, culture, society, the environment, and economics are some of the aspects that come into play when thinking about the impact of visitor behavior on sensitive sites. This is a subject that is constantly evolving. It is a difficult task to strike a balance between satiating the curiosity of tourists and ensuring that they behave in a polite and culturally aware manner while also conserving the historical and cultural authenticity of these sites.

It is imperative that stakeholders place a priority on responsible engagement and sustainable tourism practices in light of the fact that sensitive sites continue to attract people in search of education, introspection, and connection with history and culture. We can ensure that these areas continue to be places of remembrance, education, and respect for future generations of people by successfully navigating the ethical problems that are involved with visitor conduct at sensitive sites.

4.3 Balancing education, remembrance, and entertainment

The protection of history, the encouragement of commemoration, and the provision of educational opportunities are all significantly aided by the existence of sensitive places such as memorials, historical landmarks, museums, and other cultural institutions. Visitors are able to connect with the complexity of human history and culture by visiting these locations, which frequently function as a bridge between the past and the present. However, striking a balance between educational opportunities, memorialization, and recreational pursuits at these sites presents a number of complex challenges. This investigation dives deeper into the complexities of this delicate balance by investigating how sensitive locations negotiate the realms of education, recollection, and entertainment while facing a variety of ethical, cultural, and practical constraints. Specifically, this investigation looks at how memorials and museums deal with the challenges of balancing education, remembrance, and entertainment.

1. **The Importance of Vulnerable Locations**
   Keep the past alive and well
   In their capacity as stewards of history, sensitive sites are responsible for preserving the recollection of past occurrences, whether they were happy or sad. They offer tourists a direct connection to the past and make it possible for them to interact with history in a manner that cannot be replicated by reading about it in a book or watching a documentary.
   Foster a sense of remembrance
   The memory of historical events, sacrifices, and the tales of persons who were engaged must be kept and perpetuated in order for sensitive sites to fulfill one of its fundamental responsibilities, which is to ensure that this memory is maintained. The process of remembering is essential to developing a knowledge of how the past influences both the present and the future.
   Inform Those Who Pay a Visit
   Visitors have the opportunity to gain knowledge about history, culture, and the human condition through the use of sensitive sites, which are extremely effective instructional instruments. They make it easier to share knowledge, thoughts, and understanding with others.
   Arouse the Feelings
   When they visit historically significant locations, people frequently experience a range of feelings, from solemn introspection and profound loss to feelings of inspiration. The emotional connection that people have with their past and their culture is what these sites aim to tap into.
   Help to Promote Dialogue
   Conversation and discourse about the past, the present, and the future can be encouraged at historically sensitive sites. They serve as a forum for conversations pertaining to historical occurrences, contemporary challenges in society, and the protection of cultural heritage.
2. **The Struggle to Strike a Balance Between Education, Memorialization, and Entertainment**
   Expectations of the Visitors
   Visitors to sensitive locations bring a wide variety of expectations with them. Others may be searching for a more immersive or fun experience, while yet others may be interested in gaining a deeper education. Site operators have a responsibility to accommodate the varied preferences of visitors.
   Considerations Regarding Both Culture and Ethics
   The planning and administration of sensitive areas are affected by the cultural norms and ethical issues that are present. What one culture deems to be courteous and suitable behavior may not be the same as what another culture considers to be respectful and proper.
   The Truth About the Economy

There are a lot of sensitive sites that rely on cash from tourists to keep their doors open. It might be difficult to strike a balance between the requirements of maintaining the site's integrity while also ensuring its continued financial viability.

The Influence That It Has On One's Emotional Well-Being

Sites that are deemed sensitive have the potential to provoke powerful feelings in visitors, who may have varying emotional responses to the same sight. The management of the site are obligated to take the potential psychological toll of the visitors into consideration.

Permanence and Safeguarding of Resources

It can be difficult to strike a balance between the requirement for conservation and preservation and the desire to accommodate tourists. Having a large number of visitors can cause wear and tear, which is why proper management is required.

3. ### The Provision of Education at Vulnerable Locations
   #### Contextualization of the Past

Historically sensitive sites typically provide extensive historical context. Exhibits, objects, and narratives that provide a full understanding of the events that are being celebrated are sometimes featured in museums.

The Recording and Presentation of Events

The activities or persons connected to the place are documented and communicated through the use of original sources such as photographs, papers, and diaries, among other primary sources.

Exhibits That Encourage Interaction

Many environmentally sensitive locations feature interactive exhibits as a way to get people involved and improve the quality of their learning experience. Touchscreens, audio guidance, and even virtual reality experiences could be among these technologies.

Programs for Instructional Purposes

Educational opportunities such as lectures, workshops, and guided tours could be available at historically significant locations. These programs make it possible to have a more in-depth interaction with the historical or cultural value of the location.

Signs With Explanatory Notes

Visitors can be provided with historical background, context, and insights into the value of the place through the use of interpretative signage that has been thoughtfully developed. These signs are meant to be used as aids in schooling.

4. ### Commemoration at Historically Significant Locations
   #### Observance of the dead

Memorialization can be accomplished in a variety of ways, including the construction of physical memorials such as statues and plaques, as well as the performance of symbolic acts such as the burning of candles or the placement of flowers.

The Peace and Quiet of Being Alone

The practice of observing intervals of silence and seclusion, which provide opportunities for individual contemplation and remembering, is encouraged at many sensitive places.

Events Devoted to Commemoration

For the purpose of commemorating significant anniversaries or providing chances for communal remembering, certain delicate locations play host to memorial services and other types of commemorative gatherings.

The Process of Providing Testimony

The memories and experiences of people connected to the site are frequently presented to visitors, and they are frequently urged to share their own testimony. Remembering anything includes one of its most important components: bearing witness.

Care and Maintenance of Artifacts

Another significant aspect of remembering a location is ensuring that any artifacts or historical items connected to the location are carefully preserved. These relics are important because they provide a direct link to the past.

5. **Amusement at Secret or Sensitive Locations**

    Totally Submerging Adventures

    Some environmentally sensitive locations provide tourists with fully immersive experiences that take them to another era or location. These encounters have the potential to be both educative and enjoyable at the same time.

    Presentations of Audio-Visual Material

    Engaging historical or cultural narratives can be communicated through the use of audiovisual presentations such as documentaries, films, or virtual reality installations.

    Presentations of Various Cultures

    Cultural acts, such as music, dancing, or theater, can provide an entertaining and cultural component, which can enrich the experience that visitors have while they are there.

    Activities That Involve Interaction

    The visit may be made more interesting and entertaining through the participation of the visitor in interactive activities, such as art installations or hands-on exhibitions.

    Narrative That Is Captivating

    The entertaining potential of a sensitive location can be increased through the use of a compelling narrative or storytelling method. Visitors can be captivated and history can be made more accessible by carefully constructing narratives.

6. **Obstacles to Overcome and Ethical Conundrums**
   Accessibility versus Archival Preservation
   There may be instances when the need to make sensitive places available to a wide audience is in direct opposition to the wish to preserve those sites. Large numbers of visitors can cause wear and tear, which puts the site's physical integrity at risk.
   The practice of business
   The process of commercializing sensitive places can compromise both their authenticity and the historical relevance of those locations. The quest of financial gain can sometimes result in the trivialization of serious matters.
   Influence on the Feelings of Those Who Visit
   A difficult and intricate task lies in the management of the emotional influence on the tourists. Although the purpose of sensitive websites is to elicit feelings, designers must also take into account the risk of emotional excess.
   Respect for Different Cultures
   Respect should be shown for both cultural standards and customs. It is possible that behavior that is acceptable in one culture could be considered disrespectful in another society.
   Expectations of the Visitors
   The expectations of guests can differ significantly. It is an ongoing challenge to find a happy medium between the competing goals of providing an experience that is both immersive and engaging while also meeting the demand for in-depth instruction.
7. **Techniques for Striking a Balance Between Education, Commemoration, and Entertainment**

There are a few different approaches that can be taken in order to traverse the complications of striking a balance between teaching, commemoration, and entertainment at sensitive sites.

Design That Is Focused On The Customer
The visitor should always be considered during the planning process of sensitive places. This includes the creation of displays that are interesting and engaging, as well as elements that are interactive and signage that is easy to understand.

Education That Covers Everything
It is important for educational opportunities in historically or culturally significant locations to be extensive, so that tourists can gain a profound comprehension of the surrounding environment. This can include making use of primary sources, going on tours led by experts, or visiting immersive exhibitions.

Competence Across Cultures

When it comes to maintaining sensitive locations, cultural knowledge is absolutely necessary. The management of the site ought to have a solid understanding of the cultural mores and sensitivities associated with the location.

Support on an emotional level

Visitors to sensitive locations should be given the opportunity to get emotional assistance, as they may find the experience to be upsetting. This may involve having access to resources such as counseling or assistance.

Tourism Methods That Are Friendly To The Environment

The management of tourist behavior and the preservation of the natural integrity of sensitive sites are both critically dependent on the implementation of sustainable tourism principles. In order to accomplish this goal, it may be necessary to restrict the number of visitors, strictly enforce the rules, and place an emphasis on conservation.

Commercialization with a Sensible Attitude

In the event that commercialization is required to ensure financial viability, approaching it with caution is strongly recommended. It is the responsibility of the managers of the property to guarantee that the cultural and historical significance of the location is not diminished for financial gain.

At sensitive places, finding a happy medium between educating visitors, honoring past events, and entertaining visitors is a difficult task. These locations are extremely important for the maintenance of history, the encouragement of commemoration, and the provision of educational opportunities. To strike this delicate balance takes thoughtful design, cultural fluency, and an in-depth understanding of what visitors anticipate from their experience.

The obstacles and ethical conundrums that are associated with sensitive sites are numerous; nevertheless, solutions to these problems can be found through the implementation of responsible commercialization, cultural sensitivity, and sustainable tourism practices. We can ensure that these sites will continue to act as links to the past by properly monitoring the conduct of visitors and conserving the integrity of the sites themselves. This will allow people to connect with the diverse and rich fabric that is human history and culture.

Chapter 5

Commercialization and Controversy

Commercialization, which refers to the process of introducing a product or service for the purpose of making a financial profit or gain, is present in virtually every facet of contemporary life. Commercialization is a powerful force that shapes industries, economies, and individual decisions in a society that is driven primarily by consumers' desires. On the other hand, it is frequently accompanied with controversy, which can spawn debates regarding its effects on culture, ethics, the environment, and other related topics. This in-depth investigation dives into the complex relationship between commercialization and controversy in the modern world, covering a variety of topics such as advertising, technology, art, and the environment, amongst others.

1. **The opening statement**
   The process of introducing a good or service with the purpose of making a financial profit or gain has come to be known as commercialization. Commercialization has emerged as one of the defining characteristics of the contemporary world. It has an impact on every aspect of our lives, from the goods we purchase and the forms of entertainment we partake in to the services we make use of and the information we have access to. The impact of commercialization can be seen across multiple domains, including ethics, culture, and the economy.
   On the other hand, controversy frequently comes in the wake of the ubiquitous presence of commercialization. It is sometimes difficult to differentiate between satisfying the requirements and wishes of customers and taking advantage of them. The process of commercialization can give rise to moral conundrums, ignite discussions on the impact on culture and the environment, and produce tensions between profit and the general welfare of society.
   This investigation digs into the intricate and multidimensional dynamics that underlie the connection between commercialization and contentiousness. This article investigates the many facets of commercialization and the debates that it

sparks in the contemporary world. As a result, it offers some insights into the ways in which commercialization influences public discourse and how it affects our daily lives.

2. **The Everywhere Presence of Commercialization**
   Advertising and the Culture of Consumer Goods
   Advertising is one of the features of commercialization that is both the most noticeable and the most ubiquitous. It permeates every aspect of our day-to-day lives, from print media and television to social media and beyond. Advertising is intended to influence consumer behavior, leading to the development of a culture of consumerism that not only contributes to economic expansion but also creates concerns regarding society and ethical norms.
   The philosophies of Consumerism and Materialism
   The culture of getting and consuming goods and services is encouraged by commercialization, which is also known as consumerism. Some people believe that this culture is to blame for the rise of materialism since it teaches people that their worth and identity are determined by the things they own.
   The Artifice of Satisfying Cravings
   In order to generate interest in a brand's products or services, advertising will frequently employ persuasion strategies. The emergence of controversy results from the perception that these strategies are manipulative or misleading.
   Technology and the Commercialization of Digital Goods
   The dawn of the digital age marked the beginning of a fresh period of increased commercialization. Advertising revenue is used by many IT companies to support the provision of cost-free services, such as social networking platforms and search engines. The gathering of user data and the subsequent monetization of that data have given rise to discussions over privacy, surveillance, and the morality of digital commercialization.
   Data Confidentiality and Commercialization
   Concerns regarding privacy have been brought to light as a result of the gathering and selling of personal data by internet businesses. The possibility for the exploitation of data has been brought to light by scandals such as the one involving Facebook and Cambridge Analytica.
   Control and Monopolies in the Digital Age
   Tech behemoths such as Google and Amazon have come under investigation due to the dominating effect they have on respective industries. Competition in the market, antitrust rules, and equitable economic treatment are some of the topics at the center of the debate.
   The Performing and Visual Arts
   The fields of art and entertainment have struggled with commercialization for a very long time. The desire of financial gain can occasionally come into conflict with maintaining artistic integrity and preserving cultural significance.

The appropriation of culture
When it comes to the arts, commercialization can sometimes lead to cultural appropriation, which is when elements of one culture are appropriated and commercialized by another culture. This brings up concerns regarding ethics, respect, and representation in the workplace.

The Influence That Commercialism Has On Creative Freedom
The desire of financial gain has the potential to impact creative decision-making in the entertainment sector. When artistic freedom is sacrificed in order to serve commercial goals, there has been a surge in the number of controversies around this issue.

The Rise of Consumer Brands in an Age of Globalization
The expansion of commercial activity on a worldwide scale has resulted in the proliferation of consumer brands in many parts of the world. Controversies arise when the standardized products that multinational firms develop for worldwide markets are incompatible with the local customs and cultures of certain countries and regions.

The homogenization of cultures
Global companies frequently promote a standardized consumer culture, which can be detrimental to the preservation of regional customs and values. Some people think that this will lead to a loss of cultural diversity and an increase in cultural sameness.

Resistance on a Local Level to Global Brands
There is a possibility that local communities will put up a fight against the expansion of global companies in order to promote the protection of their distinct cultural heritage. This conflict between global brands and regional identities frequently gives rise to contentious debate.

3. **The Moral Conundrums that Come With Commercialization**
Because the goal of profit can often collide with larger society ideals and beliefs, commercialization is riddled with ethical difficulties that must be navigated carefully. The process of commercialization gives rise to a number of different ethical considerations.

Mistreatment of Workers, Including Exploitation and Other Abuses
The pursuit of profit can often result in the exploitation of workers, which is especially common in industries such as fast fashion. There is much debate on the working conditions and pay levels of people employed in global supply chains.

Environmental Repercussions and Long-Term Viability
The commercialization of goods and services can put a strain on the natural world due to excessive consumption, waste, and behaviors that are not sustainable. These controversies revolve primarily around discussions over climate change, the depletion of resources, and the ecological footprint left by commercialization.

Deception of Customers and Attempts to Manipulate Them
There are occasions when the persuasive strategies employed in advertising and marketing surpass the boundaries of what is ethical. Consumers' perceptions that they are being controlled or misled by commercial methods can give rise to contentious debates.

Both Privacy and Surveillance are Important
In this day and age, the gathering of private information and the monitoring of internet activity have given rise to moral concerns over individuals' right to privacy. It has recently come to light that there is a lot of controversy regarding data breaches as well as the usage of personal information for financial gain.

Responsibility to the Community and Ethical Business Practices
There are moral conundrums that arise from the social responsibilities of corporations. Companies that put a greater emphasis on profit than they do on social or environmental problems are seen as having questionable business ethics. The debate includes topics such as ethical sourcing, fair trade, and the duty of corporations to their communities.

4. **Commercialization and Contentious Debates Regarding Culture**
The cultural debates that have arisen as a result of commercialization are varied and touch on a variety of topics, including concerns of identity and representation as well as cultural values. The process of commercialization gives rise to a number of significant cultural problems.

The appropriation of culture
When aspects of one culture are taken and used by another culture, typically without the former culture's permission, this is an example of cultural appropriation. When people view this form of appropriation in a manner that is disrespectful or damaging, controversy ensues.

Concerning Representation as well as Stereotyping
Commercialization, especially in the media and advertising, can contribute to the perpetuation of damaging stereotypes or the misrepresentation of a variety of cultural groups. Questions of representation and their effect on people's worldviews are at the center of controversies.

The Safekeeping of Our Cultural Traditions
Concerns regarding the protection of cultural heritage can be raised when cultural artifacts and practices are put up for sale on the market. Authenticity, commodification, and the preservation of cultural integrity are frequently at the focus of contentious debates.

Resistance on a Local Level to Globalization
It is possible for cultural tensions and resistance to arise as a result of the expansion of global brands into local communities. There is a possibility that local inhabitants will make an effort to save their cultural identity against the impact of commercialization.

5. **The Impact of Commercial Activity on the Environment**
The environmental debates that are sparked by the commercialization of a resource are important and have far-reaching implications. The behaviors of commercial enterprises frequently put a strain on natural resources, are a contributor to pollution, and undermine the ecological equilibrium.
Waste and excessive usage of goods
Overconsumption and the production of a large quantity of trash are both consequences of consumerism, which is pushed by commercialization. This topic is at the forefront of discussions concerning environmental stewardship and long-term sustainability.
Consumption of Resources
The harvesting and consumption of natural resources, such as water, minerals, and forests, can have severe negative effects on the surrounding ecosystem. Concerns have been raised about the effects of resource depletion on the surrounding environment.
Pollution as well as the Degradation of the Environment
Commercialization is one of the primary contributors to environmental degradation, including contamination of the air and water as well as the destruction of habitats and forests. Concerning who exactly is responsible for fixing these environmental problems—companies or governments—there are many different schools of thought.
The Changing Climate and Emissions of Carbon
The widespread commercialization of products and services, in particular in sectors such as the transportation and energy industries, is a contributor to the generation of carbon dioxide and the progression of climate change. There is a lot of debate about whether or not commercialization is to blame for the worsening of global environmental problems.

6. **The Part Played by the State and Its Regulations**
When it comes to handling the controversies that are involved with the process of commercialization, the government and regulatory organizations play a significant role. They do this by passing laws and regulations to govern business operations and safeguard the rights of customers, workers, and the environment.
Regulations for the Protection of Consumers and Advertisers
Advertising standards and consumer protection regulations are overseen by many regulatory authorities. They labor to guarantee that advertisements do not engage in deceptive practices and that customers are educated about the rights and options available to them.
Regulations Regarding the Environment
Environmental agencies and laws both have the goal of reducing the negative effects of business activities on the environment. They provide guidelines for emissions, the disposal of trash, and the management of resources.

Laws Governing Labor and Employment
The purpose of laws governing employment and labor is to shield workers from being exploited or forced to work in hazardous situations. They discuss topics like as the minimum wage, working hours, and the safety of the workplace.

Laws Regarding Antitrust and Competition
Laws designed to prohibit monopolies and other unfair business activities in the market are called antitrust and competition laws. They watch out to make sure that consumers are not put in danger or that competition is not hampered by commercialization.

7. **The Prospects for Commercialization and the Continued Existence of Controversy**

There is little reason to expect that the connection between commercialization and contentious debate will weaken over the next few years. In point of fact, new types of commercialization and the conflicts that are linked with them are expected to develop as technology continues to advance and the global economy continues to evolve.

Commercialization of Digital Technologies
The influence of the digital age will continue to be seen in the commercial sector. E-commerce, social networking, and advertising that is driven by data will continue to be at the forefront of digital commercialization, which will ignite fresh discussions about privacy, surveillance, and the ethics of conducting business online.

Concern for the Environment and Ethical Consumption
The importance placed on environmentally friendly practices and moral shopping will have an effect on commercialization. Businesses will need to modify their policies in order to remain competitive as customers become increasingly aware of the ethical and environmental consequences of their purchasing decisions.

Control and Administration of Regulations
It is anticipated that the government's control and regulation of commercial practices will become more stringent. Regulatory agencies will play a vital role in tackling these issues as long as the conflicts around data privacy, environmental sustainability, and ethical concerns continue to be a focal point.

Diversity in Cultural Expressions and Representation
The contention that there should be more cultural representation and diversity will continue to be a central issue in cultural debate. As societies become increasingly varied and linked, the commercialization of cultural objects and practices will come under increased scrutiny for the effect it has on individuals' identities and how they are represented.

Responsibility Towards the Environment
The importance of quickly tackling climate change and the destruction of the environment will continue to have a formative influence on the debates that surround commercialization. customers will have a favorable opinion of businesses that place a

priority on sustainability and environmental responsibility, while customers may have a negative opinion of businesses that do not.

Commercialization is a distinguishing feature of the modern world; it influences not just economies and civilizations but also individual decisions. However, its ubiquitous presence is accompanied with a wide range of contentious debates and discussions. The difficulties that arise between profit-driven motivations and the general well-being of society are reflected in the ethical conundrums, cultural worries, and environmental arguments that are brought up by commercialization.

It is crucial to find a balance between economic growth and the preservation of ethics, culture, and the environment as we negotiate the complexities of commercialization and the debates that it causes. This is especially important as we work our way through the complications of commercialization. The future of commercialization will be characterized by advances in technology, increased regulation, and an ever-increasing emphasis on responsible and sustainable business practices. In the years to come, one of the most important challenges will be to master the complexities of commercialization and the debates that surround it.

5.1 The commodification of dark tourism

In recent years, there has been a meteoric rise in the popularity of a subgenre of the travel business known as "dark tourism." This form of tourism centers on locations that are connected with tragic events and places of human misery. The commercialization of dark tourism presents a number of difficult ethical problems, despite the fact that it affords one-of-a-kind chances for education and introspection. This investigation digs into the difficulties and debates that surround the commercialization of dark tourism. Topics covered include questions about ethics and authenticity, as well as the delicate balancing act that must be performed between making a profit and engaging responsibly with sensitive areas.

1. **The opening statement**

    Dark tourism, a word that was first introduced by Lennon and Foley in the year 2000, is a form of tourism that entails going to locations that are connected with death, sorrow, pain, or historical events that are frequently gloomy or macabre. The concentration camp Auschwitz in Poland, the Hiroshima Peace Memorial in Japan, the Chernobyl Exclusion Zone in Ukraine, and Alcatraz Island in the United States are some of the attractions that fall under this category. Dark tourism presents visitors with one-of-a-kind chances to learn about history, ruminate on the breadth and depth of the human experience, and come face to face with the shadowy sides of our nation's past.

    However, there is rising worry over the commercialization of dark tourism as a result of this trend. The boundary between responsible and exploitative behaviors has become increasingly blurry as a direct result of the growing demand for these kinds of experiences. This investigation digs into the commodification of dark tourism, exploring both the ethical conundrums and the authenticity issues that arise, as well as the delicate balance that must be struck between making a profit and engaging responsibly with sensitive areas.

2. **The Expansion of Unsanctioned Travel**
   The Media and the Culture of Pop
   The popularity of films, documentaries, and television series that investigate mysterious or historical occurrences has led many people to become interested in traveling to the corresponding locations. The films "Schindler's List" and "The Chernobyl Diaries" are responsible for bringing attention to locations that are connected with misery and suffering.
   Having Educational Importance
   Many people are drawn to gloomy tourism destinations out of a sincere desire to learn and achieve a more profound comprehension of the historical events that took place there. These locations frequently function as essential teaching aids, allowing visitors to better comprehend the importance of times gone by.
   Connection on an Emotional Level
   Dark tourism has the potential to arouse a range of feelings, from serious thought to compassion for those who were afflicted. Visitors take away a deeper sense of meaning from their encounter as a result of these emotional connections.
   Opportunities to Travel More Regularly
   It is now more simpler for tourists to visit dark tourism areas since improvements have been made in terms of accessibility, transportation, and technology. The travel industry as a whole, including tour operators and agencies, has benefited from this trend.

3. **A Consideration on the Morality of Commercialization**
   Take advantage of
   The pursuit of profit can result in the exploitation of environmentally vulnerable areas. The drive for financial gain can easily obscure the importance of remembering and respecting the past.
   The pursuit of sensuality
   Some forms of commercialization place more of an emphasis on dramatic or morbid characteristics, which has the potential to make the pain that occurred in the past seem less significant. This kind of sensationalism has the potential to come across as impolite and improper.
   Infrastructure Dedicated to Tourism
   The establishment of tourist infrastructure near sensitive sites has the potential to upset the surrounding communities and to transform the nature of these locations. This has led to concerns being expressed regarding the maintenance of the site's authenticity and the effects on the people who live there.
   Disparity in the Economy
   There is not always a fair distribution of the financial gains that come with dark

tourism. There is a possibility that local communities will not receive their due part of the earnings, which will result in economic inequalities.

4. **Authenticity and the Tourism of Dark Places**
When it comes to the business side of dark tourism, authenticity is one of the most important concerns. The goal of visitors to these locations is to have experiences that are genuine and meaningful, however the presence of commercialization can occasionally impair authenticity.

Storytelling in its Pure Form
Destinations that are part of the dark tourism industry are obligated to provide genuine and correct narratives of the historical events they portray. This involves making use of primary documents, historical context, and the direction of subject matter experts in order to guarantee that visitors receive an all-encompassing education.

Finding a Happy Medium Between Authentic and Commercial Interactions
The careful balance that must be maintained between commercial activity and genuine relationships is essential for the success of dark tourism destinations. Authenticity is at risk if profit is prioritized over other considerations.

Maintaining the Architectural Consistency of Sites
Commercialization typically results in an increase in the number of visitors, which can impose stress on the psychological and physical integrity of sensitive places. The authenticity of these locations must be protected at all costs by preserving the historical and cultural relevance of the locations in question.

5. **Finding a Happy Medium Between Making a Profit and Being Responsible**
Finding a happy medium between making a profit and being responsible is one of the primary challenges of the dark tourism industry. Engaging responsibly with these websites calls for vigilant management to ensure that monetary advantage does not come at the expense of ethical considerations.

Control and Administration of Regulations
In order to effectively control the commoditization of dark tourism, governmental authorities and site managers need to establish legislation and mechanisms for oversight. This includes enforcing ethical norms, imposing restrictions on the number of visitors allowed, and safeguarding the sites' integrity.

Marketing That Is Responsible
The successful and ethical promotion of dark tourism is largely dependent on the efforts of tour operators and travel companies. Ethical marketing strategies make certain that the experiences are portrayed in a manner that is both true and courteous.

Concentration on Education
At dark tourism destinations, placing an emphasis on education can assist in maintaining a responsible balance between profit and ethics. These websites may

place an emphasis on teaching and remembering at the expense of sensationalism and financial gain.

Equality in Economic Terms

It is of the utmost importance to ensure economic fairness. It is imperative that local communities and stakeholders receive benefits from the marketing of dark tourism, and that existing economic inequities be remedied.

6. **The Part That Travel Agencies and Tour Operators Play in the Industry**

The successful commercialization of dark tourism is largely due to the contributions made by tour operators and travel agencies. They are accountable for striking a balance between profit and ethical concerns in all of their decisions.

Educational Trips and Visits

Educational tours that give guests a thorough comprehension of the historical setting can be fashioned by tour operators in a way that caters to their needs. Learning and introspection are emphasized during these journeys.

Respect for Different Cultures

It is crucial to have cultural awareness. Tour operators have a responsibility to educate themselves about the cultural mores and sensitivity issues associated with the destinations they market.

Marketing That Is Responsible

The organizers of tours are obligated to engage in appropriate marketing practices that provide a truthful portrayal of the activities available at tourist destinations with a sad history. It is best to steer clear of marketing tactics that are exploitative and sensationalist.

Collaborating with the Neighborhoods and Communities

It is essential to collaborate with the local community and the many stakeholders. It is possible for tour operators to collaborate with the local community in order to ensure that the economic benefits are fairly distributed.

Dark tourism is a substantial and expanding area of the tourist business that provides one-of-a-kind possibilities for introspection and education. The commodification of dark tourism, on the other hand, poses a host of difficult ethical problems. It is absolutely necessary, in order to maintain the originality and integrity of these delicate locations, to strike a responsible balance between making a profit and acting ethically.

It is necessary for tour operators, governments, and site managers to collaborate in order to guarantee that dark tourism will continue to have an educational emphasis, will be respectful of cultural sensitivity, and will be beneficial to local communities. By balancing the obstacles of commercialization with a dedication to responsible engagement, dark tourism can continue to function as a platform for learning, contemplation, and remembering while also addressing the ethical dilemmas that are brought about by the phenomenon.

5.2 Marketing and branding of morbid attractions

When it comes to the promotion and commercialization of morbid attractions, marketing and branding play an essential part. Morbid attractions are a subset of dark tourism that focuses on death, tragedy, and the macabre. In recent years, there has been a rise in the appeal of these attractions, which include locations such as catacombs, haunted houses, and tours of genuine crime sites. However, there are a number of difficult ethical problems raised by the marketing and branding of macabre attractions. This investigation dives into the problems and debates that have arisen as a result of the commercialization of these attractions. Topics covered include questions of ethics and authenticity, as well as the thin line that separates making a profit and engaging in macabre activities in a responsible manner.

1. **The opening statement**
   A broad audience that is looking for experiences that are one of a kind and out of the ordinary has taken an interest in morbid attractions, which are a subset of dark tourism. These attractions cover a wide variety of locations and pursuits that are in some way connected to macabre themes like death and sorrow.
   Those who are interested in the macabre can indulge their curiosity at a variety of morbid attractions, such as catacomb tours, ghost tours, and visits to actual crime scene locations.
   Marketing and branding have become essential components of the industry in response to the growing demand for these types of experiences. The manner in which macabre attractions are promoted and given their names has a huge impact on the way in which the general audience experiences and views them. However, its commercialization is not without criticism, and it raises ethical difficulties surrounding respect, authenticity, and the balance between making a profit and not exploiting the sensitive character of these attractions.
2. **The Multiplication of Sickly Attractions**
   The Influence of Pop Culture
   Audiences have been drawn by television dramas, movies, and books that center on genuine crimes, the supernatural, and historical tragedies. People's interest in horrific destinations has been stimulated thanks to these types of media, which has led to an increase in macabre tourism.
   A need for one-of-a-kind experiences
   When going on vacation or spending their free time, a lot of people want to do things that are different from what everyone else does. Morbid attractions are a departure from traditional tourist spots, and they cater to those who are looking for something else than the same old thing.
   Exhilaration and Mysteriousness
   People are frequently drawn to macabre attractions due to their fascination with the unknown, the mysterious, and the scary. They provide a sense of surprise,

mystery, and excitement that is sometimes difficult to discover in more typical kinds of tourism.

Having Educational Importance

Visitors can frequently take advantage of educational possibilities at macabre sites, gaining insight into topics such as criminal history and local customs. Many tourists arrive with the sincere intent to learn new things and discover new places.

3. **Ethical Considerations in Advertising and Branding**

    The pursuit of sensuality

    Sensational marketing and branding strategies have the potential to demonstrate a lack of respect while also trivializing the sorrow involved with terrible situations. Using the macabre for the sake of generating shock value is something that could be considered unethical.

    The battle between commercialization and authenticity

    The issue lies in finding a happy medium between the economic objectives and the genuine atmosphere of the macabre attractions. It is unacceptable for the pursuit of profit to jeopardize the authenticity of these experiences or to mislead guests.

    Due Consideration for Touchy Subjects

    When marketing and branding morbid attractions, it is absolutely necessary to show proper deference to touchy subjects like the victims of violent crimes and tragic events in the past. The possibility of causing someone emotional hurt or contempt is at the center of ethical considerations.

    Where the Line Is Drawn Between Instruction and Recreation

    It is essential to make a distinction between an experience that is informative and one that is entertaining. There is a possibility that some attractions place a greater emphasis on entertainment than education, which raises problems regarding the obligation of these attractions to inform and educate visitors about the subject matter.

4. **Authenticity, as well as the Appeal of Macabre Attractions**

    Storytelling in its Pure Form

    Morbid attractions are required to provide tales that are genuine and truthful of the macabre or historical events that they portray. This includes utilizing historical context, primary materials, and the supervision of subject matter experts to ensure that visitors receive an all-encompassing education.

    Finding a Happy Medium Between Authentic and Commercial Interactions

    It might be difficult to successfully straddle the thin line that exists between authentic relationships and commercial activity. An excessive focus on profits might detract from the genuine nature of an event, which in turn can invite criticism.

Maintaining the Architectural Consistency of Sites
Commercialization frequently results in an increase in the number of visitors, which places stress on the attractions' capacity to maintain their physical and emotional authenticity. It is absolutely necessary, for the sake of preserving authenticity, to protect the historical and cultural relevance of these locations.

5. Socially and Environmentally Responsible Marketing and Branding

In order to successfully navigate the ethical challenges that are associated with morbid attractions, responsible marketing and branding are required.

Authentic Representation
The marketing and branding for morbid attractions should provide an accurate portrayal of the experiences that are on offer. The use of marketing tactics that are deceptive or sensational should be avoided in favor of openness.

Concentration on Education
The efforts that are put into marketing and branding should revolve around an educational objective at their heart. It is important for tourist destinations that feature macabre themes to have an emphasis on education and introspection, so that guests leave with a better comprehension of the subject matter.

Respect for Different Cultures
When it comes to marketing and branding, having cultural awareness is really necessary. It is important for companies to be aware of the cultural mores and sensitivity issues associated with the tourist destinations they market.

Collaborating with the Neighborhoods and Communities
When it comes to appropriate marketing and branding, collaboration with local communities and other stakeholders is absolutely necessary. It makes certain that the economic advantages are distributed fairly and that the effects on the surrounding community are taken into consideration.

A growing number of tourists are drawn to gruesome sites because of the attention they place on death, tragedy, and other unpleasant topics. The marketing and branding of these sites are extremely important factors in determining the kinds of experiences and impressions that are left by tourists.

It is imperative that efforts be made to successfully navigate the ethical problems that are linked with the marketing and branding of macabre attractions.

Maintaining a balance between profit and ethical considerations requires a number of critical components, including responsible marketing, an educational focus, cultural awareness, and partnership with local communities.

By resolving these moral conundrums, the tourism industry will be able to assure that macabre attractions will continue to provide one-of-a-kind and genuine encounters that are sensitive to the delicate nature of the subject matter they explore while also giving insightful learning opportunities about history and culture.

5.3 Controversies surrounding commercialized death

In today's modern culture, the practice of making a profit off of goods and services connected to death, known as "commercialized death," is becoming more and more widespread. This multidimensional phenomenon spans a variety of different industries, ranging from the macabre and the marketing of terrible events to the funeral business and memorialization of the dead. The commercialization of death, despite the fact that it presents potential for economic gain, also generates complicated problems that have ethical, cultural, and societal elements. This investigation examines into the moral conundrums and cultural obstacles that are involved with the commercialization of death. It does so by analyzing themes such as death-related items, funeral services, and the memorialization of public disasters.

1. **The opening statement**
   There has been a shift in perspective on death and the goods and services that are linked with it, which has led to the rise of a concept known as the "commercialization of death." This concept has acquired significance in modern culture. The business of death has grown to encompass a diverse array of commercial endeavors; it is no longer confined to solemn and confidential dealings alone. The emergence of new economic opportunities is concurrently accompanied by the emergence of a plethora of problems, which range from ethical considerations to difficulties relating to cultural sensitivity.
   This investigation will focus on the debates that have been sparked by the increasing commercialization of death and will investigate major facets of this multifaceted phenomena. These key components will include the selling of death-related items, the memorialization of public tragedies, and funeral services. Because of the ways in which these issues intersect with ethical, cultural, and social dimensions, there is a great amount of controversy around them in today's society.

2. **The Increasingly Commodified Nature of Funeral Services**
   The Conflict Between Commercialism and Compassion
   Some people believe that the increasing commercialization of funeral services puts profit before compassion and understanding for mourning families. These people make this argument. As a result of this, people have begun debating whether or not the funeral industry should be more considerate of the emotional needs of its customers.
   Methods of Exploitation and Abuse
   It has come to people's attention that the funeral industry engages in exploitative tactics, such as price gouging. During an already difficult time, the exorbitant expense of funerals can throw huge financial constraints on families already struggling to cope with their loss.
   Pressure to Spend More Than Necessary
   There are occasions when funeral houses encourage customers to spend more

than they should on caskets, memorial services, and other costs associated with funerals. The pressure from marketing raises questions about whether or not families are making decisions that are informed and unaffected by external pressure.

Concerns Regarding the Environment
The use of embalming processes and burial methods that require a significant amount of resources has given rise to debate on the influence that traditional burials have on the environment. Those who support eco-friendly or green burials argue for burial practices that are more environmentally responsible.

3. **Merchandise and commercialization that are associated with death**
The Drive for Profit
Some people believe that the desire to make a profit is behind the marketing of ostentatious and pricey stuff that is associated to death, which they say takes advantage of people's grief and emotional weakness.

Integrity in Sourcing
Caskets, urns, and other items associated with death might give rise to concerns regarding unethical sourcing practices and environmental impact throughout the manufacturing process. The issues of environmentally friendly production and responsible manufacturing come to the forefront.

Considerations Regarding Culture
When it comes to rituals and preferences surrounding death-related goods, various cultures have a variety of approaches. It's possible to cause offense and stir up controversy with marketing methods that ignore or incorrectly interpret cultural sensitivities.

Consumers as Vulnerable Targets
People who are grieving and their families are more susceptible to being taken advantage of by pushy salespeople, particularly when it comes to pricey goods. The issue of whether or not it is the obligation of sellers to prevent exploitative behaviors is a contentious one.

4. **Commemoration of Public Disasters and Catastrophes**
Methods of Exploitation and Abuse
Commercialization of public disasters, according to some who are opposed to the practice, can abuse the pain of victims and their families for financial gain, which would be unethical.

The Slippage Away from Authenticity
It is possible that a real recollection of the events that took place and the people who were impacted may be diminished if the commercialization of memorialization is allowed to take center stage. When the genuine aim of memorials is overshadowed by financial concerns, this can give rise to controversy.

The appropriation of culture
Sometimes the commercialization of memorialization will involve cultural

appropriation, which is when elements of one culture are appropriated by another culture and then sold for profit. This behavior has the potential to be perceived as rude and insensitive.

Inadequate Regulatory Oversight

The contentious nature of the marketing of public tragedy is exacerbated by the absence of transparent legislation and ethical principles in this area. It is frequently unclear how to strike a balance between the necessity of commemoration and the appropriate management of these occurrences.

5. **Ethical Considerations in the Context of the Commercialization of Death**
Transparency and making decisions after gathering relevant information
Transparency is an essential component of an ethical practice in the funeral industry. Accurate information should be made available to families, and they should be allowed to make decisions based on that information without being subjected to excessive influence or pressure.

Compassion and empathic understanding
Compassion and empathy are essential components of the ethical approach to dealing with mourning families. The pursuit of profit shouldn't come before meeting the psychological requirements of customers.

Responsibility and Long-Term Sustainability
Ethically required behaviors include those that are responsible and sustainable. It is important that death-related activities have as little of an effect as possible on the surrounding environment, and the manufacture of death-related goods should make ethical sourcing a top priority.

Respect for Different Cultures
When it comes to the commercialization of death, cultural awareness is absolutely necessary because different cultures have vastly varied traditions and tastes. Ethical behavior requires taking into account the sensitivities of other cultures.

6. **A Look at Things from a Cultural and Social Standpoint**

The Diversity of Cultures

The ways in which people mourn a loss and pay tribute to a deceased loved one are heavily influenced by cultural differences. Misunderstandings and a lack of sensitivity toward the cultural norms and beliefs of others are frequently the root of controversies.

Traditions and Rites Practiced in Social Settings

There is a large amount of variety in social rituals and traditions, and the commercialization of
these aspects of society can lead to disagreements on authenticity, respect, and cultural appropriation.

Influence felt by local communities

It is possible for the commercialization of services associated with death to have a substantial effect on communities. This not only involves concerns regarding the maintenance of local cultures and customs, but also economic factors must be taken into account.

Discussion in the public arena and general awareness

In order to resolve problems, it is essential to have public conversation and raise awareness of the moral and cultural implications of the commercialization of death. Promoting responsible behavior can be accomplished through advocacy, education, and open discourse.

The commercialization of death is a diverse and controversial phenomena that involves a variety of sectors, such as the marketing of death-related items and the memorialization of public tragedies. These industries range from funeral services to the marketing of death-related merchandise. Because of the ways in which these commercial operations intersect with ethical, cultural, and social dimensions, contemporary society views them as a topic worthy of substantial debate.

To successfully navigate the debates that surround the commercialization of death, one must strike a balance between profit and ethics. Considerations of ethics that are crucial include openness, compassion, ecological responsibility, and sensitivity to cultural norms. The industry can strive for a responsible approach to commercialized death by respecting cultural norms and beliefs, supporting ethical sourcing, and reducing the environmental impact. This will allow the industry to resolve the ethical conundrums and cultural sensitivities that develop as a result of marketed death.

Chapter 6

The Thrills and Chills of Dark Tourism

In recent years, there has been a rise in the practice of "dark tourism," which refers to the act of traveling to locations that are linked with morbid topics such as death, tragedy, and the macabre. The concept of "dark tourism" capitalizes on the human preoccupation with the macabre and the unexplained by providing a one-of-a-kind combination of thrills and chills that appeal to a wide variety of people. This investigation dives deeper into the many facets of dark tourism, including its historical origins, psychological allure, contemporary expressions, and the ethical conundrums that it raises. By delving into the thrills and chills of dark tourism, we are able to untangle the complexity that motivate people to investigate these eerie locations and confront the more disturbing aspects of human history.

1. **An Opening Statement Regarding the Field of Dark Tourism**
   Dark tourism, also known as thanatourism, is becoming an increasingly popular subset within the tourism business. It caters to individuals who are looking for out-of-the-ordinary and thought-provoking experiences throughout their travels. Dark tourism offers a more introspective and reflective experience than traditional tourism does, allowing tourists to engage with locations that provoke feelings ranging from solemn reflection to creepy interest. Traditional tourism tends to concentrate on leisure and relaxation more often than dark tourism does. These places, some of which were formerly used as prisons or as battlefields or as catastrophe zones or as haunted locales, possess a significant historical and cultural value, and they invite tourists to investigate the more troubling periods in human history.
2. **Historical Origins and the Development of**
   It is possible to trace the origins of dark tourism all the way back to ancient civilizations. During this time period, people traveled on pilgrimages to places of religious significance, which often included locations connected with acts of

martyrdom and sacrifice. The idea progressed throughout time to incorporate a wider range of locations, including memorials and memorialization sites dedicated to historical atrocities as well as battlefields and execution grounds. The emergence of dark tourism is a manifestation of the human yearning to know and confront the more negative aspects of human history. This desire highlights the importance of education and recollection in the process of forming our collective comprehension of the past.

3. **Psychological preoccupation with macabre subject matter**
   The potential of dark tourism to elicit a variety of emotional responses in visitors, such as empathy, dread, and curiosity, is one of the primary reasons for its popularity among tourists. The excitement of discovering areas that are cloaked in mystery and tragedy provides a one-of-a-kind form of psychological stimulation, leading tourists to reflect on the complexity of human nature and the precarious aspect of existence. In addition, the experience of confronting one's own mortality as well as the unknown frequently results in a transforming and introspective journey for many individuals who partake in gloomy tourism.

4. **Modern-Day Manifestations and In-Demand Vacation Spots**
   The modern era has witnessed a considerable increase in the appeal of dark tourism. This rise in popularity has been fueled by a growing interest in historical atrocities, true crime accounts, and the supernatural. The allure of seeing places connected with significant human experiences is demonstrated by the fact that well-known tourist spots like Auschwitz-Birkenau in Poland, Chernobyl in Ukraine, the Catacombs of Paris, and the Tower of London continue to draw millions of people each year. These places are haunting reminders of the atrocities, tragedies, and cultural occurrences that have had a role in shaping our shared psyche.

5. **Ethical Conundrums and the Responsibility of the Tourism Industry**
   Even though it provides a forum for teaching and remembering the past, dark tourism also raises a number of serious ethical questions. The task of striking a balance between the educational value of these places and the requirement for polite and appropriate involvement continues to be an important one. An approach to dark tourism that is intelligent and ethical is required since there are concerns over the sensationalization of tragedies, the impact on local communities, and the commodity of tragedies. It is imperative that responsible tourism practices be followed in order to guarantee that these locations will be protected, maintained, and presented in a manner that is respectful to the memories of those who were impacted by the events that these locations represent.

6. **The Importance of Mass Media and Conventional Culture**
   The widespread availability of media, such as televised shows, motion pictures, and documentary films, has been an essential contributor to the growth of the dark tourism industry. True crime shows, paranormal investigations, and

historical dramas have all contributed to the mainstream attraction of dark tourism. These forms of media have helped shape popular conceptions and encouraged a deeper level of engagement with the narratives linked with these locations. However, the power of the media also raises problems about the balance between accurate historical portrayal and entertaining content, highlighting the necessity of critical engagement with the narratives that are given.

7. **The Effects on Culture and Society Caused by Dark Tourism**
   Dark tourism has a significant impact not just on culture but also on society as a whole, and as a result, it often sparks discussions about collective memory, the need of preserving history, and the morality of remembering. It inspires people to contemplate the intricacies of human history, the lingering legacy of sorrow, and the resiliency of communities that have been challenged by hardship. Furthermore, it encourages a more in-depth comprehension of the sociopolitical circumstances that have played a role in molding the world, highlighting the significance of appreciating the past in order to shed light on the present and construct a future that is more empathic and well-informed.

8. **Considerations Regarding the Environment and Long-Term Sustainability**
   The growth of dark tourism has also brought the issue of environmentally responsible practices to the forefront in recent years. The protection of these historical sites, which are frequently situated in delicate ecosystems, calls for meticulous maintenance and environmentally conscious techniques in order to ensure that they will be around for subsequent generations. This requires achieving a healthy balance between the amount of visitors to these locations, implementing acceptable waste management practices, and safeguarding the ecological and cultural authenticity of these areas.

9. **Psychological Effects on Those Who Come to Visit**
   It is possible for visitors to undergo significant psychological transformations as a result of their
   involvement in dark tourism. Some people may find comfort in the time for reflection and remembering, while others may feel emotional discomfort or trauma as a result of the event. The psychological repercussions of dark tourism underscore how important it is to provide proper support and resources for visitors. These support and resources should include on-site counseling services as well as educational materials that place the experiences into a larger historical and social context.

10. **The Path Ahead for Dark Tourism: Current Trends and Potential Opportunities**

When looking into the future, it is likely that changing travel preferences, developments in technology, and shifting public views about the study of sensitive historical sites will all play a role in shaping the future of dark tourism. It is possible that the use of immersive technology such as virtual reality and augmented reality will offer new pathways for engaging with dark tourism. This would enable tourists to experience historical events in a manner that is both more interactive and educative. In addition, it is anticipated that an increasing emphasis on responsible and sustainable tourist practices will have an impact on the establishment of rules and policies that prioritize the preservation of these sites while also encouraging a deeper awareness of the value of their historical roles.

Dark tourism, which combines thrills and chills, is a monument to humanity's everlasting interest with the macabre and the unexplained, and it serves as an example of this obsession. It provides a one-of-a-kind chance for introspection, knowledge, and empathy, and it encourages visitors to confront the most troubling aspects of human history and think about the resiliency of the human spirit. A deeper appreciation for the complexities of the human experience and the significance of conserving historical memory can be fostered by appropriate participation with dark tourism, despite the fact that it raises a number of difficult ethical questions and poses difficult issues. It is essential that we approach these locations with reverence and respect and a dedication to building a more empathic and informed understanding of our collective history as we navigate the multifarious world of dark tourism. This is especially important because dark tourism is still relatively new.

6.1 Experiences and emotions of dark tourists

Dark tourism, which refers to the practice of going to locations linked with death, tragedy, and the macabre, is a one-of-a-kind form of travel that is emotionally charged. When people go to locations associated with dark tourism, they frequently find themselves on a trip that elicits a variety of feelings, ranging from somber introspection and empathy to dread and curiosity. In this investigation, we dive into the experiences and feelings of "dark tourists" and investigate the psychological and sociological aspects that contribute to their obsession with the macabre and the unknown. By diving into the thought processes of dark travelers, we are able to obtain a more profound comprehension of the intricate dynamic between curiosity, empathy, and introspection that serves as the foundation for their travels.

1. **The opening statement**

   Traveling to places linked with death, misery, and other negative emotions is an example of a subset of the tourism business known as "dark tourism." Dark tourists engage on travels that contradict the normal expectations of tourism, even though it may appear incongruous to find leisure and attraction in such areas. These tourists are drawn to destinations such as the Auschwitz concentration camp, the Chernobyl Exclusion Zone, and the catacombs of Paris because they are in search of experiences that are emotionally charged, thought-provoking, and, in some instances, genuinely uncomfortable.

   Curiosity, empathy, and a longing for one's own introspection are frequently

present components of dark tourists' experiences and feelings. "Dark tourism" refers to travel that focuses on the dark side of human nature. This investigation dives into the intricate realm of dark tourism and seeks to gain an understanding of the psychological and social causes that motivate people to investigate eerie locations and confront the more disturbing aspects of human history.

2. **Comprehending the Concept of the Dark Tourist**
The Shadowy Side of the Tourist
Many different age ranges and cultural backgrounds are represented among dark travelers. People who visit these locations could be people interested in history, people looking for thrills, academics, or people who have a personal connection to the historical events that are portrayed at these sites. The reasons someone chooses to participate in a dark tourism adventure are likely to be highly personal to them, and they will differ from traveler to tourist.
Reasons for Engaging in Dark Tourism
Educational Curiosity: Some "dark tourists" go to historical places, political landmarks, and cultural landmarks with the hopes of gaining a more in-depth comprehension of historical events, political movements, and cultural phenomena.
Emotional Connection: The emotional effect of these sites frequently leads to feelings of empathy and somber thought. The victims of these incidents may be on the minds of visitors, and they may feel obligated to pay their respects.
Fascination with the Macabre: For some people, the fundamental motivation behind their interest in these things is a fascination with the macabre and the unknown. These tourists are lured to the black tourism industry because of its creepy and mysterious qualities.
Seeking Thrills Those in search of a heart-pounding experience may be drawn to dark tourism because of the adrenaline rush that comes with touring locations that are known to elicit strong feelings and cause unease in visitors.

3. **The Emotional Range That Dark Tourism Encompasses**
Respectful Contemplation
When they visit places connected with sorrow and suffering, many dark travelers are overcome by an overwhelming sense of solemnity. These feelings may include sorrow, regret, and a profound sense of reverence for the people who perished as a result of historical occurrences. In order to show their appreciation for those who overcame adversity, visitors frequently observe minutes of silence devoted to contemplation and recollection.
Compassion and a Sense of Connection
A typical feeling shared by many dark travelers is that of empathy. Visitors frequently state that they experienced a powerful sense of connection to the people who suffered or passed away at these sites. This empathy can be a motivating force behind the desire to understand more about the events that took place and

the people who were a part of them.

Concern and apprehension

There are several tourist destinations that inspire feelings of dread and unease. It is possible for visitors to experience terror as a result of the spooky and uncomfortable ambiance of haunted locations, such as catacombs, abandoned asylums, or other locations said to be haunted. It is possible for fear to act as a potent emotional trigger that contributes an element of excitement to the experience.

Both fascinate and pique one's interest.

One of the most typical feelings experienced by "dark tourists" is a strong curiosity with the macabre and the unexplained. Their interest is fueled by a yearning to delve into the murkier corners of human history, unearth previously untold tales, and test the boundaries of the known universe. This curiosity frequently results in in-depth investigation and active participation in historical narratives.

Consideration of Oneself

The experience of dark tourism frequently provokes introspection. Visitors may find themselves pondering their own place in history, the ethical repercussions of the historical events they are investigating, and the life lessons that can be learned from looking back on the past. Reflecting on one's own experiences can frequently result in a more profound recognition of the resiliency of the human spirit as well as an increased capacity for empathy.

4. **The Importance of Storytelling and Narrative in Today's World**

Storytelling that is Both Authentic and Comprehensive

Dark tourists are interested in hearing narratives that are genuine and all-encompassing, providing them with a thorough knowledge of the events and the historical situations in which they occurred. These narratives frequently feature personal anecdotes, historical documentation, as well as help from subject matter experts.

The importance of remembering

The significance of remembering important events is frequently emphasized in the narratives provided at dark tourism sites. These narratives create empathy and a sense of duty to remember and honor the memories of those who suffered or passed away by focusing on the stories of the persons who suffered or passed away.

A Sensationalistic Check and Balance

There is a great amount of difficulty involved in striking a balance between sensationalism and responsible storytelling. Responsible storytelling strives to represent the historical and cultural relevance of the events in a manner that is respectful, despite the fact that certain aspects of dark tourism can be sensationalized for the sake of providing entertainment value.

Establishing a Connection on an Emotional Level

The most successful narratives are those that enable visitors to feel as though they are emotionally connected to the people who were actually there and experienced the events. These narratives make the encounters more meaningful by cultivating empathy as well as a sense of connection with the audience.

5. **Psychological Effects of Nighttime Travel and Tourism**
   Results That Are Favorable On The Psychological Front
   Many people who go to dark tourism destinations report having good psychological benefits, such as improved empathy, a deeper grasp of history, and a greater appreciation for the resiliency of the human spirit. These results illustrate the potential for education and empathy that can be gained from participating in dark tourism.
   Emotional Toughness and Adaptation Strategies
   Some visitors may find that engaging in dark tourism helps them build emotional resilience and improves their ability to cope with difficult situations. They are able to confront their own feelings, concerns, and anxieties, which helps them feel that they have grown as individuals as a result of their exploration of the darker sides of human history.
   Distress and Trauma on an Emotional Level
   On the other side, certain people may be more susceptible to experiencing mental anguish and trauma as a result of dark tourism. The profound feelings that are commonly connected with these locations can be overpowering, which might result in psychological difficulties that call for support and techniques for coping.
   The Value of Helping Others and Getting an Education
   It is imperative that support services and educational resources be made available in order to address the potential psychological effects of dark tourism. The presence of on-site counselors, instructional materials, and conscientious tour operators can all play an important part in ensuring that guests are provided with sufficient support and information.

6. **The Effects on Society and Culture Caused by "Dark Tourism"**

   Recollections from the Past
   Dark tourism is important to the preservation of collective memory since it helps to preserve tragic historical events and occurrences in the public's mind. Conversations on the duties of remembering and the lessons that can be learned from the past are prompted as a result.
   Protection of Historical Sites
   It is essential to the practice of dark tourism that historical sites and the stories associated with them be preserved. In many cases, the preservation and safeguarding of these sites is made possible by the financial benefits that are accrued as a result of the interest shown by visitors.
   Challenges of a Moral Nature

The practice of dark tourism presents a number of difficult ethical concerns, including those about responsible participation, sensitivity to the needs of local people, and the possibility of sensationalism. These predicaments highlight how important it is to strike a balance between instructive and entertaining components.

Respect for Different Cultures

When it comes to dark tourism, several civilizations have developed a variety of distinct customs and tastes. When connecting with these sites, it is essential for visitors to demonstrate cultural awareness in order to ensure that they respect local norms and traditions.

Conventional ideas about travel and tourism are pushed to their limits by dark tourism, which involves engaging in emotionally taxing encounters and engaging in a complex interplay of curiosity, empathy, and introspection. Visitors to dark tourism sites engage on experiences that provoke a wide range of feelings, ranging from serious introspection and connection to dread and interest, depending on the specific dark tourism destination. Individuals are encouraged to confront the more troubling aspects of human history and consider their place in the wider world as a result of these experiences.

The psychological and societal facets of black tourism shed light on the transformative potential of these travels while also highlighting the issues that they may present. By diving into the thought processes of dark tourists, we are able to obtain a more profound comprehension of the singular and emotionally charged qualities of the experiences they have had. In the end, dark tourism serves as a platform for inquiry, self-discovery, and empathy, forcing tourists to interact with history in a profound and thought-provoking manner.

6.2 How dark tourism fulfills a unique niche in travel

Dark tourism is a subset of the travel industry that gives tourists the option to visit locations connected with morbid topics such as death, tragedy, and the macabre. This gives dark tourism a distinct and intriguing function within the travel industry. Dark tourism, as opposed to typical tourism, which frequently places an emphasis on leisure and relaxation, caters to persons who are looking for experiences that are thought-provoking and emotionally intense. This investigation digs into the manner in which "dark tourism" fills a distinct void in the travel industry. It does so by investigating the psychological allure, educational value, and ethical considerations that lie at the root of the human obsession with the macabre and the unexplained. By delving into the intricate realm of dark tourism, we are able to discover the variables that attract tourists to these eerie locations and highlight the significance of engaging in responsible behavior while visiting these locations.

1. **A Confrontation with the Unpleasant Side of Traveling 1. Introduction:**
   Travel has long been connected with leisure activities such as exploration and relaxation, providing individuals with the opportunity to get away from the

monotony of day-to-day living and learn about new places and cultures. However, there is a subset of travelers who are looking for a different kind of voyage, one that takes them to locations that are associated with tragic events and morbid themes. This one-of-a-kind and profoundly moving mode of discovery is being catered to by a subset of the travel business called "dark tourism," which is also often referred to as "thanatourism."

The term "dark tourism" refers to a variety of different types of destinations, such as places that were formerly used as concentration camps, battlefields, crime scene locations, catastrophe zones, and haunted locations. The ability of these locations to elicit a wide range of feelings, ranging from solemn thought and empathy to intrigue and fear, is what sets them distinct from other locations. Dark tourism is a subset of the travel industry that challenges traditional ideas about tourism and encourages individuals to investigate the intricacies of the human experience. It does this by giving tourists the option to become involved with the most negative aspects of human history.

2. **The Appeal of Dark Tourism from a Psychological Perspective**

Curiosity and awe in the face of the unknown

Many times, a profound sense of curiosity about the unknowable is what compels individuals to engage in dark tourism. They go to different locations with the goal of uncovering the secrets, forgotten history, and hidden stories that are connected to those locations. A strong impetus is provided by the want to decipher the mysteries of these locations and gain an understanding of the activities that took place there.

Empathy as well as Emotional Participation

It is common for feelings of empathy and emotional engagement to be triggered by visiting areas connected with pain and calamity. Visitors who seek out dark tourism say they are struck by a profound sense of empathy with the people who were tortured or killed at the sites they visit. This empathy can be a motivating force behind the desire to understand more about the events that took place and the people who were a part of them.

The Excitement of Something Spooky and Unnerving

Thrill seekers are drawn to the spooky and unpleasant ambiance at many of the tourist destinations that specialize in dark tourism. It's possible to feel both terror and exhilaration while exploring abandoned asylums, catacombs, or other haunted locales. The experience is made more exciting by the excitement of entering into these terrifying settings, which adds a dimension of adventure.

The yearning for one's own introspection

The experience of dark tourism frequently provokes introspection. Visitors may find themselves pondering their own place in history, the ethical repercussions of the historical events they are investigating, and the life lessons that can be learned from looking back on the past. Reflecting on one's own experiences can frequently result in a more profound recognition of the resiliency of the human spirit as well as an increased capacity for empathy.

3. **Its Educational Importance and Its Significance in History**
Travelers will have the ability to interact with historical and culturally significant sites if they choose to partake in dark tourism. Dark tourism places a greater emphasis on learning and remembering than does regular tourism, which frequently places a greater emphasis on leisure and relaxation. Dark tourism fills a distinct void in the travel industry, and one of its defining characteristics is a dedication to maintaining an accurate historical record and preventing the important lessons of the past from being forgotten.

A Forum for the Commemoration and Education of the Past
Visitors are able to get a more in-depth comprehension of historical occurrences, political movements, and cultural phenomena through the practice of "dark tourism," which functions as a forum for teaching and remembering. These websites typically include in-depth narratives that shed light on the historical circumstances surrounding the events being discussed.

The Responsibility to Remember
Dark tourism places an emphasis on the responsibility of remembering. Visitors are strongly urged to pay their respects to the victims of historical catastrophes and to engage in introspection regarding the ways in which these occurrences continue to have an impact on modern society. This sense of duty helps to cultivate a deeper appreciation for the resiliency of the human spirit as well as the significance of the preservation of historical memory.

Finding a Middle Ground Between Sensationalism and Responsibility
A big obstacle is presented when attempting to strike a balance between sensationalism and responsible engagement. Responsible involvement strives to explain the historical and cultural relevance of the events in a manner that is respectful, despite the fact that certain aspects of dark tourism can be sensationalized for the sake of providing entertainment value. The educational value that may be gained from participating in dark tourism is fundamental to the distinct travel market that it occupies.

Creating a Greater Depth of Understanding
The practice of dark tourism contributes to a greater depth of comprehension regarding the geopolitical conditions that have molded the world. It starts conversations about the things that we can learn from history, the legacies that tragedies leave behind, and the resiliency of communities that have been through difficult times. The educational value of dark tourism highlights how important it is to acknowledge the past in order to better understand the present and to construct a future that is more compassionate and knowledgeable.

4. **Ethical Considerations, in addition to Responsible Participation**

Honoring the Memories of Those Who Have Passed
Respect for the memory of those who were killed or injured in past atrocities is one of the most important factors to take into account when engaging in "dark tourism." Visitors are strongly urged to interact with these locations in a way that pays respect to the memory of those who were injured or killed as a result of the events that took place here.

Finding a Happy Medium Between Learning and Having Fun
The dark tourism industry needs to find a happy medium between educating visitors and

entertaining them. Despite the fact that it is only normal for some components of these experiences to be exhilarating or even enjoyable, responsible involvement should prioritize the maintenance of historical memory and the conveyance of cultural importance.

Sensitivity to the Communities That Are Local
Locations popular for dark tourism are frequently found in close proximity to local towns. Being sensitive to the influence that tourism has on these communities, both the economic benefits as well as the potential disruptions, is a necessary component of responsible participation. It is essential to make certain that tourists behave courteously and make a constructive contribution to the economy of the area in which they are visiting.

Staying away from sensationalism as well as exploitation
Sensationalism and exploitative practices have no place in the dark tourism industry. It is essential to convey the historical events and the experiences of the persons involved in a manner that respects their humanity and dignity in order to do justice to the subject matter. These websites have the potential to educate and inspire empathy, but sensationalism and exploitation detract from that promise.

The human preoccupation with the macabre and the unknown provides a rich source of material for "dark tourism," which fills a specific void in the travel industry. Travelers will have the opportunity to explore locations connected with death, sorrow, and the unknown, which will provide experiences that are both emotionally intense and thought-provoking. Dark tourism is differentiated from regular tourism in that it challenges visitors to interact with the intricacies of the human experience by appealing to people on a psychological level, having educational value, and taking ethical concerns into mind.

As the popularity of dark tourism continues to rise, it is becoming increasingly necessary to engage in safe behavior while visiting these locations. Dark tourism fills a distinct void in the tourist industry, and travelers may fully appreciate this by engaging these experiences with reverence, respect, and a commitment to building a more empathic and informed understanding of our collective history.

6.3 The fine line between fascination and discomfort

Dark tourism, which refers to the practice of going to places connected with death, tragedy, and the macabre, frequently muddles the line between fascinating and unsettling experiences at the destinations it visits. When visiting places like Auschwitz, Chernobyl, and former prisons, tourists who partake in what is known as "dark tourism" often find themselves treading a fine line between their natural curiosity and a growing sense of uneasiness. This investigation dives deeper into the varied nature of this narrow line, analyzing the psychological components, emotional responses, and ethical considerations that lie at the foundation of the experiences of dark tourists. We reveal the deep relationship between the macabre and the mysterious by diving into the complexities of intrigue and discomfort in dark tourism. This forces visitors to confront the more disturbing aspects of human history and forces them to grow as people.

1. **An Introduction: Finding Your Way Through the Maze That Is Dark Tourism**

    In recent years, there has been a rise in the popularity of dark tourism as a response to the trend of tourists seeking out unusual and mind-bending experiences. When they travel to locations associated with death, tragedy, and the macabre, "dark tourists" find themselves walking a delicate line between being fascinated and being uneasy. The human predilection for the macabre and the unexplained is what gives rise to curiosity, while the unpleasant and gloomy quality of the locations contributes to the discomfort that people feel when visiting them.

    In the course of this investigation, we will dissect the intricate relationship that exists between dark tourism's attractions and its inherent unease. We dive into the psychological characteristics that attract tourists to these locations, investigate the emotional responses that they elicit, and traverse the ethical conundrums that these locations present. By doing so, we obtain a deeper knowledge of the varied character of dark tourism, which encourages visitors to explore the complexity of the human experience and confront the darker chapters of history. Dark tourism exists where there is a narrow line between curiosity and discomfort, and it is in these places that travelers can find themselves.

2. **The Appeal of Dark Tourism from a Psychological Perspective**
    Curiosity and awe in the face of the unknown

    Curiosity for the unknowable is one of the fundamental psychological aspects that folks are drawn to when participating in dark tourism. The visitors to these locations are interested in solving the mysteries that surround them, including the hidden histories, stories, and legends that are associated with them. The appeal of understanding the secrets of these sites is a powerful incentive, frequently motivating deep inquiry and involvement with the narratives that are presented.

Empathy as well as Emotional Participation
The psychological attractiveness of dark tourism can be broken down into several components, one of which is empathy. Visitors frequently state that they experienced a powerful sense of connection to the people who suffered or passed away in these locations. Because of this empathy, one feels compelled to discover more about what happened and the people who were involved, which in turn leads to solemn meditation and the act of remembering.

The Seeking of Thrills and the Spooky
Thrill-seekers, who are often drawn to dark tourism because of its appeal to their sense of adventure, are drawn to the spooky and unpleasant qualities of the sites they visit. It's possible to feel both terror and exhilaration while exploring abandoned asylums, catacombs, or other haunted locales. In these settings, when there is a heightened sense of excitement for guests, the thin line that separates fascinating and unsettling is especially obvious.

The yearning for one's own introspection
The experience of dark tourism frequently provokes introspection. Visitors may find themselves
pondering their own place in history, the ethical repercussions of the historical events they are investigating, and the life lessons that can be learned from looking back on the past. Reflecting on one's own experiences can frequently result in a more profound recognition of the resiliency of the human spirit as well as an increased capacity for empathy.

3. **Emotional Reactions to Haunted Attractions in Tourism**

Respectful Contemplation and Compassion
When they visit places connected with sorrow and suffering, many dark travelers are overcome by an overwhelming sense of solemnity. These feelings may include sorrow, regret, and a profound sense of reverence for the people who perished as a result of historical occurrences. In order to show their appreciation for those who overcame adversity, visitors frequently observe minutes of silence devoted to contemplation and recollection.

Concern and apprehension
There are several tourist destinations that inspire feelings of dread and unease. It is possible for visitors to experience terror as a result of the spooky and uncomfortable ambiance of haunted locations, such as catacombs, abandoned asylums, or other locations said to be haunted. The fear component is a big contributor to the delicate balance that exists between being fascinated and being uncomfortable, which adds a dimension of excitement to the experience.

Both fascinate and pique one's interest.
One of the most typical emotional responses exhibited by dark tourists is a sense of curiosity with the macabre and the mysterious. Their interest is fueled by a yearning to delve into the murkier corners of human history, unearth previously

untold tales, and test the boundaries of the known universe. This curiosity frequently results in in-depth investigation and active participation in historical narratives.

Transformation and introspection of oneself
Traveling to darker parts of the world can frequently provoke introspection and personal growth. The visitors are encouraged to reflect about their own mortality, values, and place in the world while they are there. Individuals are forced to confront their own thoughts and feelings as a result of this self-reflection, which is an essential component of the thin line that separates intrigue and discomfort.

4. **Ethical Conundrums and the Duty to Engage in Responsible Behavior**

Finding a Happy Medium Between Learning and Having Fun
The delicate balancing act between educational opportunities and recreational pursuits is one of the most significant challenges presented by dark tourism. Despite the fact that it is only normal for some components of these experiences to be exhilarating or even enjoyable, responsible involvement should prioritize the maintenance of historical memory and the conveyance of cultural importance.

Sensitivity to the Communities That Are Local
Locations popular for dark tourism are frequently found in close proximity to local towns. Being sensitive to the influence that tourism has on these communities, both the economic benefits as well as the potential disruptions, is a necessary component of responsible participation. It is essential to make certain that tourists behave courteously and make a constructive contribution to the economy of the area in which they are visiting.

Staying away from sensationalism as well as exploitation
Sensationalism and exploitative practices have no place in the dark tourism industry. It is essential to convey the historical events and the experiences of the persons involved in a manner that respects their humanity and dignity in order to do justice to the subject matter. These websites have the potential to educate and inspire empathy, but sensationalism and exploitation detract from that promise.

Keeping alive the memories of the past
Participating in "dark tourism" in a responsible manner places an emphasis on the maintenance of historical memory. Visitors are urged to commemorate those who perished in historical atrocities and to consider how these events continue to have an impact on modern society. This dedication to remembering is an essential part of responsible tourism and should not be overlooked.

5. **A View from the Perspective of a Dark Tourist**

Expectations and Reasons Behind Our Actions
Many things, including educational inquiry, emotional engagement, fascination with the macabre, and thrill-seeking, can lead people to go on dark tourism adventures.

Their anticipations may differ, but the majority of people look to walk the narrow line between being fascinated and being uncomfortable in the hopes of having an experience that is both emotionally taxing and thought-provoking.

Transformation of the Self and Progress in Life

Some "dark tourists" find that walking the thin line between being fascinated and being uncomfortable is the path that leads to their own personal development and evolution. Because of the emotional and psychological impact of these experiences, individuals may be prompted to examine their own views and values, which can lead to a deeper understanding of what it means to be human.

Problems, as well as Ethical Conundrums

Travelers of the dark often find themselves in difficult situations and moral conundrums. They have to navigate the intense emotional terrain of these locations while maintaining a respectful attitude toward the victims' memories and the cultural weight of the occurrences. The thin line that separates fascinating and unsettling experiences can be a wellspring of inner conflict as well as a window of opportunity for introspection.

The intricate landscape that these visitors explore is reflected in the narrow line that exists between fascinating and unsettling experiences in the field of dark tourism. Conventional ideas about travel are challenged by dark tourism, which encourages travelers to investigate the intricacies of the human experience and come face to face with the worst chapters of history.

To fully appreciate the one-of-a-kind qualities of this market sector, it is essential to have a firm grasp on the psychological allure, emotional reactions, and ethical concerns associated with dark tourism. Individuals are encouraged to engage with history in a meaningful and thought-provoking manner in order to build a deeper awareness of the many facets of the human attraction with the macabre and the unexplained. The thin line that separates interest from discomfort urges individuals to engage with history in this manner.

Chapter 7

Dark Tourism and Pop Culture

Dark tourism, which refers to the habit of visiting locations connected with death, tragedy, and the macabre, has been gaining more and more importance in recent years in popular culture. Dark tourism has emerged as a topic that people all over the world find fascinating and entertaining for a variety of reasons, including movies and television series, books, video games, and social media. This investigation dives deeply into the complex relationship that exists between "dark tourism" and popular culture, analyzing the myriad of ways in which these two spheres interact with one another, have an effect on one another, and reflect the human preoccupation with the macabre and the unexplained. By analyzing the way in which dark tourism is portrayed in mainstream media, we can obtain a deeper comprehension of the factors that have contributed to the phenomenon's rise to prominence as a pervasive and persistent component of modern culture.

1. **Introductory Remarks on the Merging of Dark Tourism and Popular Culture**
   Over the past few decades, there has been a rise in the number of people interested in participating in a form of tourism known as "dark tourism." This type of vacation involves traveling to locations connected with morbid topics such as death, tragedy, and the macabre. At the same time, it has emerged as a significant facet of contemporary popular culture. The human fascination with the macabre and the unknown is reflected in the prevalence of the concept of "dark tourism" in popular culture, such as in films, television series, books, video games, and social media. This investigation deconstructs the complex link that exists between dark tourism and popular culture by analyzing the ways in which these two spheres interact with one another, have an impact on one another, and contribute to the attraction of the macabre.

   The incorporation of dark tourism into popular culture exemplifies the many facets that contribute to its attraction. It doesn't matter if the audience was exposed to it through fictitious narratives or through real-life events; either way, it managed to captivate their imagination. In the following sections, we will investigate several facets of the presence of dark tourism in popular culture by analyzing its representation in various forms of media, including film, television, literature, and the digital sphere. By analyzing these images in the media, our goal is to gain an understanding of how dark tourism has evolved into a pervasive component of today's culture and how it reflects the complex relationship that we have with the more sinister portions of human history.

2. **"Dark Tourism" in Film: From the Horror Genre to Historical Films**
   Locations from Real Life That Have Been Featured in the Movies
   On the big screen, these real-life tourist destinations have been brought to life thanks to the production of a number of movies that were shot on location there. For instance, the concentration camp known as Auschwitz-Birkenau was used as a backdrop in the movie "Schindler's List," which offered a stark contrast to the historical narrative.

   Tales of Terror and Suspense from the World of Fiction
   When it comes to the genre of horror movies, creepy tourist attractions frequently play a vital role in the story. Stories of the macabre and the supernatural are best told in places like derelict jails, haunted asylums, and other places that have been ravaged by natural or man-made disasters. Movies like "The Shining" and "The Conjuring" have helped to foster the notion that haunted tourism is inherently associated with supernatural experiences.

   Examination of the Past and Contemplation of Its Significance
   In contrast to horror films, there are movies that exploit haunted tourist attractions as a setting for historical investigation and introspection. Films such as "Schindler's List" and "The Pianist" offer powerful depictions of historical events and highlight the significance of remembering the past and being aware of its complexities.

3. **The Impact of Dark Tourism on the Small Screen: Documentaries and Television Shows**
   Documentaries and the Reality of the Nighttime Tourism Industry
   Documentaries such as "Dark Tourist" and "World's Most Scenic Railway Journeys" have been increasingly popular because they provide viewers with a first-person perspective on the experiences of tourists who travel to dark tourism locations. The emotional responses and educational components of dark tourism are examined through the lens of real-world situations in this series.

   The Art of Blending Fact and Fiction in Scripted Shows
   The plots of scripted television episodes frequently involve visits to haunted or macabre tourist attractions. Blending reality and fiction to create an atmosphere of mystery and suspense, television shows such as "American Horror Story" have

included elements of real-life haunted tourism destinations into their fictitious narratives.

Striking a Balance Between Entertainment and Learning

When depicting dark tourism, television has the ability to strike a healthy balance between entertaining viewers and educating them. Some presentations place a greater emphasis on the thrill and excitement of visiting these sites, while others place a greater emphasis on the historical relevance and the importance of remembering.

4. **A Look at the Role of "Dark Tourism" in Published Works: From Fact to Fictional Thrills**

Memoirs and Accounts of Non-Fictional Events

A great number of authors have written non-fiction essays and memoirs about their experiences traveling as people of color. These publications offer a first-person viewpoint on the emotional responses, educational value, and ethical issues involved in visiting these sites, and they describe those emotions in detail.

Speculative Cases of the Chills and Thrills

In works of fiction, the concept of "dark tourism" has consistently been one of the most prominent themes. In thrillers, mysteries, and historical novels, the macabre and the unknown frequently take center stage. These locations have been employed by authors as settings for their stories. This pattern is best demonstrated by works of fiction such as "Inferno" by Dan Brown and "The Haunting of Hill House" by Shirley Jackson.

An Examination of the Ethical Conundrums

The moral quandaries that come with dark tourism are explored in depth in a few pieces of literature. The authors encourage readers to consider the thin line that separates fascinating and unsettling topics, so drawing attention to the obligations of remembering the past and participating in the present in a responsible manner.

5. **A Look at Haunted Attractions in the Online World, Including Social Media and Video Games**

The Experience of Being a Tourist in the Digital Age Social Media

The use of social media platforms has become an increasingly common way for "dark tourists" to record and discuss their travel experiences. On social media platforms such as Instagram and YouTube, tourists share photographs, films, and written accounts of their experiences at dark tourism locations. These posts offer a virtual look into the emotional and educational facets of these travels.

Video Games and the World of Virtual Reality

Players are now able to interact with dark tourism destinations thanks to the incorporation of these locales within the storylines of video games, which provide them the opportunity to explore these areas. Games like "Resident Evil" and "Silent Hill" have taken traditionally spooky tourist destinations and turned them into the backdrop for terrifying and exciting stories.

Finding Your Way Through Ethical Conundrums in the Digital Age
Additionally, ethical problems regarding responsible participation in dark tourism are brought up by the internet sphere. The manner in which these websites are displayed and consumed online has prompted conversations about the obligations of content authors as well as consumers. There is a thin line between being fascinated and being uncomfortable with these websites.

6. **Unsavory Tourism and Its Commentary on Society**

As a Mirror for the Attitudes of Society
The depiction of dark tourism in popular media is a reflection of how society feels about death, tragedy, and the macabre. It exemplifies the intricate dynamic that exists between curiosity and discomfort, as well as the human urge to confront the past.

Increasing People's Knowledge of the Past
The participation of popular culture in dark tourism has the potential to increase historical awareness as well as the act of remembering. People who watch or read movies, television shows, books, or play video games are given the opportunity to learn about historical events and the moral conundrums that surround the sites of these events.

Invoking Controversial Ethical Considerations
When depicted in popular culture, the thin line between fascinating and uncomfortable forces viewers and readers to address ethical questions related to the responsible engagement in dark tourism. It opens up a conversation about the obligations that travelers, content authors, and the media have when it comes to displaying these sites.

Because of the way in which it intersects with popular culture, dark tourism has firmly established itself as an enduring and varied component of modern civilization. The human fascination with the macabre and the unexplained is reflected in the fact that dark tourism has the ability to captivate the imagination of people all around the world through mediums such as film, television, literature, social media, and video games. The way in which gloomy tourism is portrayed in popular culture provides us with a prism that enables us to investigate the complexities of the human relationship with death, tragedy, and the past.

It is anticipated that the dark tourism industry's impact on popular culture will continue to be strong as it continues to develop and attract more interest. The thin line that separates fascinating and unsettling experiences, as shown in popular culture, encourages consumers to reflect on the nuances of their own responses to these locations and sparks conversations about the obligations that visitors and producers have with one another. The popularity of "dark tourism" in popular culture is evidence of the ongoing fascination of the macabre as well as the potential of this aspect to both capture us and question our conceptions of how the world works.

7.1 The representation of dark tourism in literature, film, and television

The concept of "dark tourism," which refers to the act of visiting locations that are linked with death, tragedy, and the macabre, has made its way into works of fiction, films, and television shows, and has become a recurrent motif in popular culture. This investigation explores into the complex ways in which dark tourism is portrayed in these forms of media, focusing on how it is portrayed in non-fiction, fiction, documentaries, and fictional tales. We can obtain insight into the ways in which literature, film, and television have reflected and shaped our interest with the macabre and mysterious by analyzing the ways in which different kinds of narrative have engaged with the concept of dark tourism.

1. **An Introduction to the Concept of "Dark Tourism" and How It Has Influenced Popular Culture**
   Not only has the phenomena known as "dark tourism," which is based on people's innate predilection for the macabre, made its way into the world of actual travel, but it has also made its way into the worlds of fiction writing, filmmaking, and television. This combination demonstrates how areas connected with death, tragedy, and the unknown continue to hold a certain attraction over time. The representation of dark tourism in different mediums reveals the intricacies of our relationship with the macabre and the unknown.
   This investigation focuses on the depiction of dark tourism in written works, motion pictures, and television shows. It analyzes the presence of this concept in both fictional and non-fictional narratives. By doing so, our goal is to get an understanding of the ways in which the aforementioned types of narrative overlap with and contribute to the allure of dark tourism. The next sections will explore the various ways in which literature, film, and television have engaged with this idea. This is done to highlight the multifarious nature of our fascination with the macabre.
2. **Accounts and Memoirs of Non-Fiction: Real-Life Adventures in the Dark Tourism Industry**
   Individualized Expeditions Into Uncharted Territory
   Many tourists have written non-fiction descriptions of their travels to dark tourism places, in which they detail their personal experiences, emotional reactions, and thoughts following their excursions to these locations. The tales in question frequently place an emphasis on the instructive and compassionate components of dark tourism.
   Perspectives on the Past and Their Cultures
   Accounts that are not works of fiction as well as memoirs look into the historical and cultural relevance of dark tourist locations. They offer readers a more in-depth understanding of the circumstances, people, and happenings that are associated with these locations.
   Engaging in Responsible Activities While Keeping Ethical Considerations

in Mind

Authors frequently investigate the moral conundrums presented by dark tourism, prompting readers to ponder the obligations of travelers and content makers in presenting these locations in a manner that is both respectful and informative.

3. **Fictional narratives, which blur the lines between fact and fiction by incorporating elements of both**

    The Best in Suspense and Mysteries

    Dark tourism is commonly used as a setting for stories that are both intriguing and mysterious. Fictional stories that take place in these settings, such haunted asylums or abandoned prisons, try to elicit anxiety and tension while connecting with the macabre and the unknown.

    Novels Based on History

    Some works of fiction adopt a historical point of view, utilizing locations popular with the dark tourism industry as settings for their historical novels. These narratives frequently place an emphasis on the significance of remembering the past and being aware of one's surroundings, and they do so by pulling inspiration from actual events and settings.

    The supernatural and fantastical elements in science fiction

    In the domain of science fiction and the occult, one may frequently find an examination of the more sinister aspects of dark tourism. These storylines might explore into supernatural encounters, alternative realms, or futuristic interpretations of these landmarks, which would add levels of depth to the picture of dark tourism.

4. **Documentaries and docuseries serve as visual representations of real-life experiences.**

    Personal Reflections and Observations Based on Actual Events

    Documentaries and docuseries provide a visual and audio experience of dark tourism, allowing viewers to witness the emotional responses and reflections of visitors in real time. This type of tourism is also known as "dark tourism."

    Content that is both instructive and thought-provoking

    The educational value of dark tourism has been the subject of numerous films and docuseries, which, among other things, offer historical background, expert insights, and thought-provoking storytelling.

    Problems, as well as Ethical Conundrums

    These visual representations frequently investigate the moral conundrums that are posed by dark tourism, drawing attention to the obligations that are placed on travelers as well as those who are responsible for producing material about these locations.

5. **The Dark Side of Tourism on the Small Screen of Television**

    Documentaries as well as reality television

Documentaries such as "Dark Tourist" and "World's Most Scenic Railway Journeys" have become increasingly popular in recent years. These shows provide viewers an insider's perspective on the adventures that tourists have while visiting dark tourism locations. These programs provide perspectives from real life on the emotional responses and educational facets of dark tourism.

The Art of Blending Fact and Fiction in Scripted Shows

The plots of scripted television episodes frequently involve visits to haunted or macabre tourist attractions. For example, television programs such as "American Horror Story" have intertwined parts of real-life haunted tourism destinations into their fictitious tales. This combination of fact and fiction generates mystery and tension in the viewer.

Striking a Balance Between Entertainment and Learning

When depicting dark tourism, television has the ability to strike a healthy balance between entertaining viewers and educating them. Some presentations place a greater emphasis on the thrill and excitement of visiting these sites, while others place a greater emphasis on the historical relevance and the importance of remembering.

6. **The Moving Picture Industry and the Gloomy Side of Travel on the Big Screen**

Locations from Real Life That Have Been Featured in the Movies

On the big screen, these real-life tourist destinations have been brought to life thanks to the production of a number of movies that were shot on location there. For instance, the concentration camp known as Auschwitz-Birkenau was used as a backdrop in the movie "Schindler's List," which offered a stark contrast to the historical narrative.

Tales of Terror and Suspense from the World of Fiction

When it comes to the genre of horror movies, creepy tourist attractions frequently play a vital role in the story. Stories of the macabre and the supernatural are best told in places like derelict jails, haunted asylums, and other places that have been ravaged by natural or man-made disasters. Movies like "The Shining" and "The Conjuring" have helped to foster the notion that haunted tourism is inherently associated with supernatural experiences.

Examination of the Past and Contemplation of Its Significance

In contrast to horror films, there are movies that exploit haunted tourist attractions as a setting for historical investigation and introspection. Films such as "Schindler's List" and "The Pianist" offer powerful depictions of historical events and highlight the significance of remembering the past and being aware of its complexities.

7. **The Role of Digital Platforms in the Development of "Dark Tourism" in the Digital Age**

The Experience of Being a Tourist in the Digital Age Social Media

The use of social media platforms has become an increasingly common way for "dark tourists" to record and discuss their travel experiences. On social media platforms such as Instagram and YouTube, tourists share photographs, films, and written accounts of their experiences at dark tourism locations. These posts offer a virtual look into the emotional and educational facets of these travels.

Video Games and the World of Virtual Reality
Players are now able to interact with dark tourism destinations thanks to the incorporation of these locales within the storylines of video games, which provide them the opportunity to explore these areas. Games like "Resident Evil" and "Silent Hill" have taken traditionally spooky tourist destinations and turned them into the backdrop for terrifying and exciting stories.

Finding Your Way Through Ethical Conundrums in the Digital Age
Additionally, ethical problems regarding responsible participation in dark tourism are brought up by the internet sphere. The manner in which these websites are displayed and consumed online has prompted conversations about the obligations of content authors as well as consumers. There is a thin line between being fascinated and being uncomfortable with these websites.

8. **The Influence of Representation: The Function of Dark Tourism as a Social Critique**

As a Mirror for the Attitudes of Society
The depiction of dark tourism in these forms of media is illustrative of the sentiments that exist among society regarding death, tragedy, and the macabre. It exemplifies the intricate dynamic that exists between curiosity and discomfort, as well as the human urge to confront the past.

Increasing People's Knowledge of the Past
The participation of popular culture in dark tourism has the potential to increase historical awareness as well as the act of remembering. People who watch or read movies, television shows, books, or play video games are given the opportunity to learn about historical events and the moral conundrums that surround the sites of these events.

Invoking Controversial Ethical Considerations
Audiences are challenged to address ethical considerations connected to responsible engagement with dark tourism by the depiction of a delicate line between interest and discomfort in literature, film, and television. This line forces audiences to think about the ethics of responsible participation with dark tourism. It opens up a discussion about the obligations that travelers, content authors, and the media have when it comes to responsibly portraying these locations.

It is a monument to the enduring fascination of the macabre and its potential to capture and challenge our view of the world that the depiction of dark tourism in many forms of media such as literature, film, and television exists. The concept of dark tourism never ceases to enthrall and resonant with people all over the world, no matter if it is presented in the form of non-fiction tales, fictional narratives, documentaries, or scripted shows.

The intricacy of the concept of dark tourism is reflected in the multifarious nature of the representation of dark tourism. It acts as a platform for research, education, and empathy, while also challenging folks to examine their own attitudes to these sites. It is likely that the depiction of dark tourism in popular culture will continue to have an impact, molding the way in which we interact with the most ominous aspects of human history as well as the fascination of the macabre and the unknown as the industry continues to develop and garner continuous interest.

7.2 How popular culture influences our perception of morbid attractions

The manner in which we understand and interact with macabre tourist destinations is profoundly influenced by popular culture. These kinds of attractions, which include ghastly entertainment, strange curiosities, and horrific tourist destinations, have become increasingly common in our culture. This investigation investigates how movies, television, literature, social media, and other kinds of entertainment impact our fascination with the macabre by delving into the intricate relationship that exists between popular culture and morbid inclinations. Insight into the ways in which these cultural phenomena both reflect and challenge our relationship with death, the mysterious, and the morbid can be gained by analyzing the role that popular culture plays in shaping our perspective of morbid attractions. This can be done by focusing on how these cultural phenomena influence our perception of morbid attractions.

1. **A Brief Introduction Regarding the Influence of Popular Culture 1.**
   Popular culture, which is sometimes defined as the cultural aspects that are pervasive in everyday life, plays a vital part in the process of forming both our views and the things that interest us. This effect extends to our preoccupation with macabre attractions, which cover a broad spectrum of activities and encounters associated to death, tragedy, and the macabre. These landmarks are now well established in our cultural environment, and the popular culture that surrounds them serves as both a mirror for and an influence on them.

   In this investigation, we take a look at how the influence of popular culture might shape how we think about macabre attractions. We investigate how death and the macabre are portrayed in various mediums, including film, television, literature, and social media. We look into the ways in which cultural phenomena not only reflect our preoccupation with the macabre but also present us with new challenges regarding our perception of it. The next sections investigate the myriad of ways in which popular culture influences our interaction with macabre attractions and how we react to them.

2. **The Meaning of Death in Film and the Influence of Visual Narrative The Genres of Horror and Thriller**

The horror and thriller subgenres are frequently the entry point for our interest with the macabre in popular culture. Movies that deal with paranormal occurrences, people who commit serial murders, and locations that are said to be haunted have the ability to terrify and suspense their audiences. The viewers are introduced to creepy and unnerving aspects of death and the unknown through the medium of these flicks.

Films of a dramatic and documentary historical nature
Film has the ability to educate audiences about historical happenings and the macabre attractions that were associated with them. Cinematic storylines that investigate the bleak periods of history may be found in movies like "Schindler's List" and "Hotel Rwanda," amongst others. They do this in order to educate us and challenge our notions of actual morbid attractions in the world.

A Speculative Look at the Horror Travel Industry
Movies frequently employ real-life tourist attractions as the backdrop for their made-up plots. These storylines, like "The Shining" and "The Conjuring," combine fact and fiction to create experiences that are both exhilarating and thought-provoking. This portrayal not only entertains, but also influences how we think about these locations.

3. **The Influence of the Small Screen on Gruesome Attractions on Television**
Documentaries as well as Investigations of Actual Events
Documentaries such as "Dark Tourist" and "World's Most Scenic Railway Journeys" give viewers a first-person perspective on the experiences of tourists who visit macabre sites. The emotional responses and educational features of these attractions are examined via the lens of real-world viewpoints provided by these series.

Adapted Performances and Works of Fictional Narrative
Television shows that are scripted frequently include gory or otherwise disturbing elements in their narratives. The television show "American Horror Story" is a good example of this, as it incorporates parts of real-life macabre attractions into its fictitious plots. The fact that it's hard to tell what's real and what's made up undermines our impression of these locations.

Striking a Balance Between Entertainment and Learning
In its presentation of macabre attractions, television has the ability to strike a healthy balance between entertainment and teaching. Some presentations put more of an emphasis on the thrill and excitement of visiting these places, while others put more of an emphasis on the historical relevance and the necessity of remembering.

4. **Literature is the exercise of imagination and discovery through the use of words.**
Memoirs and Accounts of Non-Fictional Events
Non-fiction books and memoirs written by authors detail the authors'

encounters with macabre attractions and the feelings they evoked. These narratives give readers an insider's look at the feelings elicited by these attractions, as well as their educational value and ethical implications.

Novels of fiction and short story collections

In the realm of fiction, there are many different methods to investigate macabre attractions. Novels classified as "thrillers," "mysteries," and "horror" frequently make use of these types of attractions as important components of their stories. Novels such as "Inferno" by Dan Brown and "The Haunting of Hill House" by Shirley Jackson are great examples of this current literary trend.

Novels Set in the Past and Fiction Based on Real People

Some novelists like to situate their stories in historical locations that feature macabre charms. These stories, which are sometimes based on true events and circumstances, frequently place an emphasis on the significance of remembering the past and having an awareness of its complexities.

5. **"The Digital Realm: Morbid Attractions in the Age of Social Media"; "The Digital Realm"**

The Experience of Being a Tourist in the Digital Age Social Media

Individuals have the ability to capture and share their encounters with macabre attractions through the utilization of social media platforms such as Instagram and YouTube. Travelers share their experiences of the emotional and educational facets of these landmarks through photographs, films, and written accounts of their time there.

Websites and other forms of online community

People that have a peculiar interest in macabre tourist destinations can participate in internet communities and visit specialized websites that cater to their needs. These platforms offer visitors the chance to share their experiences and thoughts, in addition to providing information and discussion forums.

Video Games and the World of Virtual Reality

The tales of video games frequently involve macabre attractions, and they also provide players the opportunity to interact with these settings in some way.

Games like "Resident Evil" and "Silent Hill" take macabre attractions and reimagine them as the backdrop for terrifying and exciting narratives.

6. **Putting our preconceptions to the test: macabre allures in contemporary popular culture**

Ethical Conundrums and the Duty to Engage in Responsible Behavior

Discussions about engaging with morbid attractions in a responsible manner are prompted when popular culture depictions of ethical conundrums are brought up. This sheds light on the duties that travelers, content providers, and the media have to uphold in order to present these attractions in an educational and courteous manner.

There Is a Thin Line Between Being Fascinated and Being Uncomfortable

When it comes to engaging with macabre attractions, popular culture frequently investigates the thin line that separates fascinating and unsettling experiences. This conflict compels audiences to confront their own responses to the locations, which in turn prompts them to engage in self-reflection and address ethical issues.

The shared responsibility between producers and consumers

Our understanding of macabre tourist destinations is shaped in part not only by those who produce but also by those who consume popular culture. It is the responsibility of the creators to provide these attractions in a responsible and informative manner, while it is the responsibility of the consumers to engage critically with the content they come across.

Popular culture is an ever-evolving force that not only reflects but also molds our understanding of macabre tourist destinations. We investigate the many facets of our love with the macabre through a variety of types of entertainment, including films, television shows, books, online social networks, and other forms of media. This continual conversation pushes us to confront the most troubling parts of human existence, which in turn encourages introspection and contemplation of ethical issues.

The depiction of morbid attractions in popular culture will continue to have an impact as long as these attractions continue to develop and draw interest. The influence that popular culture has on how we understand these attractions underlines the ever-present appeal of the macabre and the unknown. It is a monument to the complicated relationship that we have with death, catastrophe, and the unknown, and it invites us to explore the limits of our comprehension and curiosity.

Chapter 8

Behind-the-Scenes of Dark Tourism

Dark tourism, which refers to the practice of visiting locations that are linked with death, tragedy, and the macabre, possesses a magnetic fascination that transcends beyond the scope of the visitor experience. This investigation will take you behind the scenes of dark tourism, diving into the intricate procedures, preservation efforts, and ethical issues that make it feasible for these attractions to exist. We explore the lesser-known aspects of black tourism at locations ranging from the past to the present, shedding light on the nuances that lie beneath the surface. These locations range from historical places to modern hotspots.

1. **An Introduction: Revealing the Secrets of the Underground Tourism Industry**
   The term "dark tourism" refers to a phenomena that extends beyond the obvious and mysterious experiences that tourists have throughout their trips. Behind the scenes of macabre tourist spots is a convoluted web of activities, preservation initiatives, and ethical considerations that are necessary to the proper operation of these places. This investigation aims to bring to light the hitherto unknown facets of black tourism by providing an in-depth look at the myriad of components that, when brought together, make it feasible for these attractions to exist. The behind-the-scenes features of dark tourism are just as diverse as the attractions themselves, ranging from historical places that bear testimony to the darkest episodes in human history to current destinations that pander to a growing fascination in the macabre. This trip behind the scenes provides us with the opportunity to investigate the inner workings, obstacles, and conflicts that help define this one-of-a-kind form of travel and remembering.
2. **The Management and Upkeep of Historical Sites in the Interest of the Preservation of Dark History**
   The Conservation Value in Addition to the Historical Significance

The purpose of preserving historical places such as Auschwitz-Birkenau, Ground Zero, and the Killing Fields of Cambodia is to serve as a witness to the past and to ensure that the events themselves are never forgotten. In order to preserve these places' original state, it is generally necessary to engage in intensive conservation activities.

Striking a Balance Between Tourism and Conservation
Finding a happy medium between accommodating visitors' needs and protecting the area's rich history is one of the most critical challenges presented by the dark tourism industry. Ongoing efforts are made to conserve sensitive locations, manage the amount of visitors to the site, and enforce stringent preservation criteria.

Ethical Considerations involved in the Act of Preserving
When it comes to protecting tourist destinations that have a sad history, ethical problems arise. Should sites always be open to the public, or is there a limit beyond which access should be restricted to respect the dignity of the departed and ensure the psychological well-being of those who visit?

3. **The Operational Machinery: Tourism Sites That Are Currently Unavailable**
Managing Customers and Tickets for an Event
The act of selling tickets and keeping track of the total number of guests is quite necessary in order to provide a secure and instructive experience. A number of methods, including as timed entries, online bookings, and visitor caps, are utilized in order to manage the crowds.

Providing Interpretation and Guided Tours
When it comes to giving context and interpretation, the most important role that guided tours perform at places frequented by dark tourism is. Visitors are assisted by knowledgeable advisors in comprehending the historical significance of the location as well as the stories it harbors.

Protection and Precautionary Measures
Because of the sensitive nature of these locations, taking appropriate precautions for security and safety is of the utmost importance. The operations of the site cannot function well without the presence of security personnel, surveillance systems, and emergency plans.

4. **Educational Initiatives: Providing Information to Visitors Regarding Our Troubled History**
Museums and Public Displays of Art
Numerous destinations for dark tourism include museums and exhibits that present the subject matter in an in-depth manner. The educational value of the experience is typically increased by the presence of objects, photographs, and personal anecdotes in these exhibits.

Programs for Education and Community Engagement
Destinations for dark tourism frequently organize educational programs and

community outreach attempts to engage with local schools, colleges and universities, and the general public. These projects hope to encourage a more in-depth comprehension of the historical occurrences and the consequences they had.

Accuracy and Integrity in Historical Research

It is vitally important to preserve the accuracy and integrity of historical records. Behind the scenes, there is a large component consisting of efforts to fact-check information and provide real historical accounts. This helps to ensure that visitors obtain information that is accurate and objective.

5. **The Function of Neighborhoods When It Comes to Coexisting With Disturbing Attractions**

Participation in the Community and Support

The local community is often involved in the process of supporting and facilitating the experience of tourists and travelers. It's possible that this will require providing services, lodging, and transportation.

Influence on the Economy

Local communities have the potential to see large positive economic effects from dark tourism. The increase in tourists results in new job openings and contributes to the expansion of the local economy.

Impact Both Social And Psychological On

Living in close proximity to macabre attractions may have repercussions for a person's social life and their mental health. The persistent recollection of previous atrocities might have an effect on the mental and emotional health of these populations.

6. **Ethical Challenges and Debates: Striking a Balance Between Honoring the Past and Looking to the Future**

The Commercialization of Human Suffering

The monetization of tragedy is one area that raises ethical questions since it gives the appearance that dark tourist destinations are capitalizing on the pain and suffering of the past for financial gain. It is necessary to find a balance between the need to generate cash and the need to respect the past.

Sense of Hospitality Towards Guests

The psychological effect that black tourism has on tourists is an important factor to take into account. Websites have a responsibility to consider the mental health of visitors who choose to engage with disturbing or tragic content.

Visitation That's Cause for Controversy: Should Certain Sites Remain Closed?

There are others who believe that particular locations should be kept off-limits to the public in order to maintain respect for the people who have passed away there. This discussion sheds light on the moral conundrums that come with dark tourism.

7. **The Importance of Technology in Providing an Improved Experience for Visitors**

   The back-end processes of dark tourism are becoming increasingly reliant on various forms of modern technology. The experience that a visitor has at a museum is being improved by technology developments such as virtual reality and interactive exhibitions.

   Both Virtual Reality and Augmented Reality are Available.
   Visitors are able to immerse themselves in historical events through the use of virtual reality and augmented reality experiences, which provides them with a deeper understanding of the past.

   Apps and Displays That Are Interactive
   Visitors are able to explore at their own leisure thanks to interactive exhibitions as well as mobile applications, which provide extra layers of knowledge as well as participation.

   Online Communities and Various Social Media
   There is a variety of information and resources that can be found on websites, social media

   platforms, and other online platforms, which are utilized to engage with visitors before and after their visits.

8. **Obstacles Facing the Dark Tourism Industry and Its Prospects**

The difficulties that arise in the planning and execution of dark tourism are always present. These problems include protecting the historical integrity of sites, striking a balance between educational and commercial interests, and addressing the ethical dilemmas that arise from the commodification of cultural goods. It is likely that the future of dark tourism will involve the development of new approaches to preservation and interpretation while at the same time continuing to struggle with the aforementioned issues.

The concept of "dark tourism" encompasses a complex realm that extends far beyond the typical tourist encounter. The work that goes on behind the scenes covers a wide range of topics, including preservation, operations, education, community engagement, ethical conundrums, and the use of technology. This investigation has shed light on previously unknown facets of gloomy tourism, drawing attention to the complexity that characterize this one-of-a-kind type of travel and commemoration.

As the world of dark tourism strives to find a middle ground between recollection and respect, education and commercial interests, historical preservation and ethical considerations, it will continue to develop and face the obstacles that it faces. It is necessary for both those who operate these attractions and people who visit them to have an understanding of the behind-the-scenes features of dark tourism. This provides insight into the complicated web that sustains this interesting and complex kind of travel.

8.1 Interviews with tour guides and operators

Dark tourism is a multifaceted phenomenon that centers on the experience of the traveler; but, at its foundation, it is brought to life by the tour guides and operators that assist travel into the macabre. In this investigation, we dig into the realm of dark tourism by conducting a series of interviews with tour guides and operators. These interviews reveal the tour guides' experiences, thoughts, and obstacles, as well as the delicate process of bringing dark attractions to life.

1. **Introduction: The People Who Work in the Shadow Tourism Industry**

   The term "dark tourism" refers to a wide variety of activities and destinations that are centered on morbid topics such as death, tragedy, and the macabre. Even while tourists come and go, the people who lead these excursions and run the businesses that provide them are what make this sector of the tourism industry so special. They serve as a link between the actual historical events, the locations where they took place, and the vacationers who are looking to gain a profound understanding of, connection to, and experience of the past.

   Within the scope of this investigation, we will be focusing on the tour guides and operators who are active within the realm of dark tourism. Our goal is to shed light on their experiences, problems, and motivations, as well as the ethical conundrums they face, through a series of interviews that we have conducted. We gain insight into the behind-the-scenes components of dark tourism as a result of hearing their voices, which enables us to comprehend the essential role performed by these individuals in molding and improving the experience that visitors have.

2. **Voices from the Frontlines, Heard Through the Eyes of the Tour Guide**
   A love for both history and the art of telling stories
   Many people who work as tour guides are interested in history and feel strongly about passing on what they've learned. They regard themselves as storytellers, bridging the gap between visitors and the past via narratives that are not only entertaining but also instructive.

   Problems of an Emotional Nature
   It can be emotionally difficult to guide visitors through locations connected with fatalities and catastrophic events. It is common for tour guides to address their own emotional responses, and they are required to offer support to customers who are profoundly impacted by what they see and do on tours.

   Considerations of an Ethical Nature
   When it comes to ethics, tour guides face challenges. They are tasked with striking a balance between the responsibilities of delivering an educational experience and the requirement of respecting the sensitivities of the site as well as the mental health of the guests.

3. **The View from Behind the Counter: Managing the Gears of the Dark Tourism Machine**
   Logistics as well as Management of the Site
   The operators are the ones who are in charge of planning the logistics of the tours, monitoring the amount of visitors, and making sure that the site is accessible while still maintaining its historical integrity.
   Merchandising and Advertising
   A careful and measured approach is required when marketing and promoting dark tourism destinations. The operators of these attractions have a responsibility to promote curiosity without giving the impression that they are trying to exploit visitors by portraying these experiences as informative and deferential.
   Taking Into Account Costs and Fees
   The pricing of tickets and the upkeep of the infrastructure are both important aspects of the finances involved in the operation of dark tourism venues. The problem of ensuring the attractions' continued profitability over the long run is a constant one.
4. **Obstacles and Ethical Predicaments: Finding Your Way Through the Gray Areas**
   Finding a Happy Medium Between Learning and Having Fun
   It can be difficult to find a happy medium between giving guests with an experience that is both instructive and entertaining while also responding to their individual interests. While some guests may view dark tourism as a sort of fun, others may be more interested in gaining a profound comprehension of times gone by.
   Having Respect for the Dignity of the One Who Has Passed
   The upkeep of the departed person's dignity and the protection of the mental health of those who come to pay their respects are two primary issues. Both the operators and the guides have the responsibility of walking the thin line that separates remembering and sensationalizing.
   Visitation That Sparked Controversy
   There is ongoing discussion on the propriety of keeping particular locations off-limits to the general public due to the sensitive nature of those locations. The promotion of responsible tourism practices is frequently the responsibility of tour operators and guides.
5. **Individual Reasons and Their Influence: Why They Chose to Participate in Dark Tourism**
   Enthusiasm for Education
   Many tour guides and operators are driven to do their jobs by a profound love of history and a strong desire to impart that love and knowledge to their clients. They view "dark tourism" as an opportunity to educate the general public about pivotal moments in human history.

Connection on an Emotional Level

A number of the people who were interviewed had a personal or emotional connection to the locations where they work. They may have had members of their family killed in historical events or they may feel a profound connection to the history of a particular location.

Advocacy for the Observance of Remembrance

The work that guides and operators do is frequently viewed as a type of advocacy for remembering past events. They hold the belief that it is essential to ensure that the events of the past are not lost to time and that those who come after them learn from the experiences of those who came before them.

6. **The Path Ahead for Dark Tourism: Emerging Trends and New Developments**

Developments in the State of Technology

Virtual reality, augmented reality, and interactive exhibitions are just some of the technologies that many people anticipate becoming further integrated into the visitor experience in the coming years.

Educational Activities and Programs

It is anticipated that a greater emphasis will be placed on education within the field of dark tourism. It is expected that there will be an increase in the number of educational programs, outreach activities, and collaborations with educational institutions such as schools and colleges.

Discussions and Debates Regarding Ethical Issues

Ethical debates over dark tourism are likely to continue in the foreseeable future. The operators and leaders of tours predict that discussions over appropriate visiting, the thin line that separates education and entertainment, and the dignity of the deceased will continue.

The hidden heroes of dark tourism are the tour guides and operators who provide the information, infrastructure, and emotional support required to make these sights accessible and educative. Their perspectives, reasons for traveling, and obstacles provide a one-of-a-kind look at the complex world of black tourism.

The behind-the-scenes features of dark tourism that have been revealed through these interviews highlight the significance of responsible visiting, the maintenance of the historical integrity, and the delicate balance that must be maintained between educational opportunities and entertaining pursuits. A deeper understanding of the world's darkest periods and the human tales that lay inside them can be facilitated by tour guides and operators, who act as the bridge between the past and the present.

8.2 Insights into the management and curation of dark tourist sites

The administration and curation of haunted tourist attractions requires striking a careful balance between protecting the tourist destination's historical authenticity, offering visitors educational opportunities, and addressing any relevant ethical concerns.

In this investigation, we dig into the complex realm of managing and curating these sites, finding the behind-the-scenes work that go into preserving the authenticity of the past while also providing experiences that are meaningful and respectful for visitors. Specifically, we look at the management and curation of a site that was formerly inhabited by Native Americans.

We acquire insights into the issues, methods, and ethical dilemmas that define the administration and curation of dark tourist sites by conducting an in-depth analysis.

1. **A Brief Introduction Regarding the Importance of Efficient Administration and Curation**
   Dark tourism attractions offer historical and cultural significance, and frequently serve as heartbreaking reminders of humanity's darkest periods. These locations attract tourists because of their unique atmosphere. It is crucial to ensure that these sites are managed and curated effectively in order to guarantee that the tales they contain are conserved, honored, and communicated to visitors in a manner that is both educational and courteous. This investigation dives into the varied nature of managing and curating dark tourist sites, bringing light on the challenges and obligations involved in sustaining these historical locations. Managing and curating dark tourist sites is a relatively new field of study.
2. **Preserving and ensuring the historical integrity of the site while preserving its authenticity**
   Strategies for Conserving Resources
   The implementation of efficient conservation measures helps to ensure that the physical structures and artifacts found at these sites are preserved in their original state. For the purpose of ensuring that the historical artifacts and relics retain their original authenticity, conservationists implement practices such as repair, upkeep, and documentation.
   Reduction of Human and Other Impacts on the Environment
   Some of the more sinister tourist destinations are found in ecologically fragile areas, which call for vigilant environmental control. Site managers must give primary focus to striking a healthy balance between the effects of visitor traffic and the maintenance of natural surroundings.
   Planning for the Long Term Conservation of Resources
   The planning for the long-term preservation of these sites requires anticipating potential difficulties in the future and putting preventative safeguards into place to protect the historical authenticity of the locations. This typically involves the creation of detailed maintenance schedules as well as the application of environmentally friendly procedures.
3. **Communicating the Past and Its Significance Through Educational Experiences**
   Exhibits and Displays That Offer an Interpretive Perspective

The process of curation frequently entails the creation of interpretive exhibitions and displays that offer historical context and make it easier for visitors to comprehend the material. To make the educational experience more engaging for visitors, these exhibitions could incorporate artifacts, multimedia presentations, or interactive components.

Educational Programs and Tours Guided by Professionals

Visitors can gain a better understanding of the historical significance of these locations through the implementation of educational programs and the organization of guided tours. The provision of in-depth information and the cultivation of meaningful involvement are both significantly aided by the presence of knowledgeable guides and instructors.

Platforms for Digital and Virtual Education and Instruction

The use of digital and virtual learning platforms has become a regular practice in the curation of dark tourist sites as a direct result of the advancements that have been made in technology in recent years. Both on-site and remote visitors can take part in instructional activities that are easily navigable and immersive thanks to these platforms.

4. **The Experience of Visitors and Their Participation: Striking a Balance Between Sensitivity and Impact**

    Support and Well-Being on an Emotional Level

    The administrators of these sites typically provide emotional support tools and information to visitors in order to assist them in navigating their experiences in a manner that is both healthy and courteous. This is because the managers are aware of the possible emotional impact that visiting these sites may have.

    Interaction with Visitors and Participation from Audiences

    It is of the utmost importance to promote visitor participation with and engagement with the historical material. Visitors are able to obtain a more in-depth understanding of the significance of these locations when chances for reflection, conversation, and personal connection are made available to them.

    Ability to Participate and Accessibility

    It is vital, in order to accommodate a wide variety of visitors, to make tourist destinations as accessible and welcoming as possible. This may entail making accommodations for those who have impairments, providing literature in multiple languages, and cultivating an atmosphere that is sensitive to and respectful of different cultural traditions.

5. **Navigating Sensitive Narratives While Considering Ethical Considerations**

    Honor and Dignity Owed to the Dead and the Living

    It is of the utmost importance to ensure that both the emotional well-being of survivors and the dignity of the departed be respected. Storytelling is an important part of any site, and site managers and curators have a responsibility to approach it with empathy and cultural sensitivity in order to ensure that the narratives offered are factual and respectful.

Finding a Middle Ground Between Education and Sensationalism
It is essential to achieve a healthy equilibrium between the provision of educational opportunities and the avoidance of sensationalism. In the process of curation, historical authenticity and a comprehensive understanding should take precedence over any sort of exploitation or reduction of the significance of the events in question.

Participation in the Community and Working Together
It is necessary to engage with local communities and stakeholders to ensure that the administration and curation of dark tourist sites are aligned with the values and requirements of the community in order to guarantee that dark tourist sites are safe for visitors. Collaborative efforts encourage mutual respect and understanding, which contributes to an approach that is more thorough and ethical to the management of the site.

6. **Adopting Sustainable Practices in Order to Ensure Viability in the Long Term**
Fostering behaviors that promote the long-term viability of these destinations from both a cultural and environmental point of view is an essential component of sustainable tourism when it comes to the management and curation of dark tourist sites.

Community Development Efforts and Programs
Key to the practice of sustainable site management is the implementation of community development activities that are to the advantage of the local residents. These initiatives may include educational programs, job creation efforts, and efforts to preserve the community's cultural traditions, all of which add to the community's overall well-being.

Efforts Made Towards the Conservation of the Environment
It is absolutely necessary to use environmentally friendly methods in order to protect the natural environment that surrounds these places. The ecological integrity of the region can be protected through the implementation of conservation measures and the reduction of the ecological impact that visitor traffic has on the area.

Preservation of Cultural Resources and Advocacy for These
It is essential to the continued economic vitality of these places that advocates for the preservation of historical and cultural sites. It is common practice for managers and curators of these sites to work together with historical preservation groups and governmental entities in order to ensure that these places continue to get attention and protection.

7. **Creativity and Flexibility in the Face of Rapid Change Evolving with the Times**

Combining of Various Technologies

The incorporation of technology into the process of museum curation, such as providing visitors with virtual reality experiences, interactive exhibitions, and digital archives, not only improves the overall experience for the visitors but also encourages a more in-depth comprehension of the historical events being presented.

Instruction on Sensitivity to Culture

It is absolutely necessary to provide employees and guides with cultural sensitivity training in order to make sure that interactions with visitors are polite and welcoming to all people. When you have an understanding of a variety of viewpoints and historical circumstances, you may present stories in a way that is more nuanced and sympathetic to the audience.

The Ability to Readjust to Altering Narratives

The ongoing process of historical inquiry and discovery causes historical narratives to vary, and as a result, site managers and curators are required to adjust their techniques of storytelling to appropriately reflect these changes. For the purpose of giving visitors with a thorough understanding of the events that took place at these places, it is necessary to keep historical information accurate and to ensure that the material is up to date.

The administration and curation of dark tourist sites carry with them the weighty burden of protecting the historical authenticity of the locations, offering educational opportunities with real-world relevance, and navigating intricate moral dilemmas. Site managers and curators contribute to the continuous remembering and understanding of humanity's darkest experiences by striking a delicate balance between preservation, education, and ethical narrative. This helps to ensure that these moments are not forgotten.

Their commitment to conserving the past and cultivating meaningful experiences for visitors assures that the tales associated with these locations will continue to be relevant and powerful for years to come.

8.3 The challenges and rewards of working in dark tourism

Working in the field of dark tourism is a singular undertaking that frequently involves intense feelings. When it comes to managing and curating locations connected with death, tragedy, and the macabre, tour guides, operators, and other professionals in this sector confront a number of problems and benefits. However, these obstacles and rewards are also part of the job. In this investigation, we look into the many facets that make up the world of dark tourism. Our goal is to shed light on the difficult dynamics that persons who work in this business experience, as well as the satisfying parts that lure them to it.

1. **Introductory Remarks Regarding the Dual Characteristics of Dark Tourism**
   Dark tourism, in which visitors go to locations associated with morbid topics such as death and sorrow, has a complex nature that is both challenging and

rewarding. People who operate in this industry have to traverse this complicated terrain in order to provide tourists with experiences that are important to them while also protecting the dignity and historical significance of the sites they are working at.

The purpose of this investigation is to shed light on the difficulties and rewards that are experienced by persons who work in the field of dark tourism. We will explore the complex nature of this one-of-a-kind industry, shedding light on its emotional costs and ethical conundrums, as well as its sense of fulfillment, opportunities to teach and memorialize, and other facets.

2. **The Emotional Cost of Guiding Visitors Through Difficult History**

When one works in the field of dark tourism, they frequently have to subject themselves to the mental and emotional strain of history. The rich histories linked with these places are a challenge for those who work as tour guides, curators, and operators.

Emotional Toughness or Resistance

The ability to be emotionally resilient in the face of adversity is a big difficulty. Professionals have the responsibility of guiding guests through narratives that are deeply touching while also managing their own emotional responses to the material.

Providing Emotional Support to Visitors

When they visit a haunted attraction, tourists frequently experience a range of feelings, from regret and wrath to feelings of introspection and grief. The professionals in charge of the event need to be ready to offer psychological support and resources to the guests, some of whom may be seriously affected.

Secondary traumatic events

Those who work in dark tourism run the risk of developing secondary trauma as a result of their regular exposure to tragic stories and the emotional impact those stories have on visitors. Dealing with the emotional toll that this has taken is a continuous struggle.

3. **Ethical Conundrums: Striking a Balance Between Respect and Education**

Honor and reverence for the Dead

The key ethical challenge is to strike a balance between showing respect for the dignity of the people who have passed away and maximizing the educational potential of the site. The efforts of professionals should be directed at honoring the memories of those who suffered while also providing educational opportunities of significant value.

Sensitivity to the Feelings of the Visitors

It is essential to have a solid understanding of the psychological effect that these sites have on visitors. The experts have to think about how to communicate complex storylines without overwhelming visitors or making them feel like they are being taken advantage of.

Visitation That Sparked Controversy

An ongoing ethical argument centers on the question of whether or not certain locations should be off-limits to the general public. It is a never-ending struggle to find a way to walk the delicate line between respecting the holiness of particular locations and allowing visitors to visit responsibly.

4. **Satisfaction: Providing Instruction and Remembering**

Keeping the past alive and well

For people working in this industry, one of the most significant motivators is the possibility of preserving history and ensuring that the stories associated with these locations are not lost to time. The role of preserving history is one that professionals take great delight in playing.

Promoting Comprehension by Doing So

It is a pleasant component of the job to be able to educate tourists about the historical significance of these locations and the lessons that can be learned from them. Many experts are of the opinion that the work they do helps further humankind's comprehension of the world's history.

Promoting the importance of remembering

When one works in the field of dark tourism, one must frequently advocate for the significance of remembering important events and preserving historical sites. The professionals in this field recognize the significance of their duties in preserving historical knowledge and transmitting it to succeeding generations.

5. **Encourage an Attitude of Respect and Sensitivity Through Education and Advocacy**

Educational Activities and Programs

The professionals that operate in dark tourism might come up with educational programs and initiatives and even put them into action. These initiatives are intended to offer visitors with context and understanding, with the goal of generating an experience that is more informed and respectful.

Respect for Different Cultures

It is essential to have an awareness of and a respect for the cultural sensitivities of guests who come from a variety of backgrounds. The professionals work hard to make the environment inviting and inclusive for all of the guests who come.

Participation in the Community

The importance of working together with the surrounding communities and interested parties cannot be overstated. Professionals work to ensure that the administration and curation of these sites are in line with the priorities and expectations of the local community.

Working in the field of dark tourism is a complex effort that requires the management of emotional tolls, the confrontation of ethical difficulties, and the discovery of fulfillment in teaching and activism. The people who make the decision to work in this industry do so with a tremendous sense of responsibility because they are aware of the emotional weight and historical significance of the locations they are responsible for overseeing.

The dynamic and ever-evolving nature of the dark tourism sector is a direct result of the obstacles and benefits associated with working in the field.

Those individuals who choose to devote their careers to this one-of-a-kind style of travel and commemoration are distinguished by their ability to navigate the emotional and ethical issues that arise while simultaneously attempting to educate and memorialize.

Chapter 9

The Future of Dark Tourism

The industry of "dark tourism," which refers to the act of visiting locations linked with death, tragedy, and the macabre, is one that is dynamic and constantly changing. This investigation digs into the potential tendencies, difficulties, and possibilities that may form the landscape of dark tourism as we look toward the future. We take a look at the many different factors that will have an impact on the development of this one-of-a-kind mode of travel and commemoration in the future, such as the incorporation of new technologies, emerging places, and ethical considerations.

1. **Introduction: Looking Ahead to the Development of Dark Tourism**
   The path that lies ahead for dark tourism is littered with alluring concoctions of obstacles and possibilities. This investigation takes us on a trip through history, illuminating the patterns and dynamics that will play a significant role in the evolution of the sector in the years to come. As technology continues to improve and new locations come into existence, the sector is faced with a number of ethical conundrums and a pressing need to find a middle ground between recollection and respect. We dig into the issues that lay ahead as we look forward to the development of the dark tourism industry.
2. **The Impact of Technological Developments on the Quality of the Visitor Experience**
   Both Virtual Reality and Augmented Reality are Available
   Virtual reality (VR) and augmented reality (AR) technology have made it possible for tourists to experience historical events as if they were actually living through them. They are able to enter the past in a very real sense, which provides them with a deeper insight into the experiences of those who actually lived through these occurrences.
   Apps and Displays That Are Interactive
   Additional information and levels of involvement can be gained through the use

of interactive exhibitions and mobile applications. Visitors are free to roam at their own speed, delve further into the historical backdrop, and even take part in interactive storytelling experiences if they so choose.

Online Communities and Various Social Media

Websites, social media, and other online platforms are being utilized increasingly to communicate with visitors before to and following their trips. They provide a plethora of knowledge, opportunity for conversation and reflection, and access to a variety of resources.

3. **Educational Initiatives: The Promotion of a More Comprehensive Understanding**

   Museums and Public Displays of Art

   Numerous destinations for dark tourism include museums and exhibits that present the subject matter in an in-depth manner. The educational value of the experience is typically increased by the presence of objects, photographs, and personal anecdotes in these exhibits.

   Programs for Education and Community Engagement

   It is probable that destinations for dark tourism will intensify their efforts to engage with educational institutions such as schools and universities, as well as the larger community. A more in-depth comprehension of the historical occurrences and the effects they had can be facilitated through collaborative efforts with educational institutions and outreach activities.

   Accuracy and Integrity in Historical Research

   It is vitally important to preserve the accuracy and integrity of historical records. It is imperative that efforts be made to fact-check information, present real historical accounts, and collaborate with historical researchers in order to guarantee that visitors obtain information that is accurate and objective.

4. **New Tourism Developments and Destinations: Increasing the Scope of the Dark Tourism Map**

   Newly Unearthed Travel Hotspots

   As global awareness of and interest in these locations continues to rise, it is anticipated that new dark tourism destinations will come into existence. It's possible that tourists will look for less well-known destinations that yet have substantial historical importance.

   Current Trends in the Tourism Industry

   Dark tourism is growing increasingly popular, and current events, such as natural disasters, terrorist attacks, and pandemics, are becoming increasingly popular subjects. It's possible that people looking for a more immediate link to history will be drawn to sites associated with current tragedies.

   Protecting Our Cultural and Historical Legacies

   The protection of cultural and historical sites can also be facilitated through the practice of dark tourism. To preserve the continuation of their culture and the stories that have been passed down through the generations, communities can take pride in their historical sites and interact with visitors.

5. **Navigating the Complexities Involved in Ethical Conundrums and Responsible Engagement**

   The Commercialization of Human Suffering

   The discussion that has been going on about the commercialization of tragedies will continue. The key ethical dilemma is to strike a balance between the imperative to increase profits and the imperative to show due regard for the past.

   Sense of Hospitality Towards Guests

   The psychological effect that black tourism has on tourists is an important factor to take into account. Websites have a responsibility to consider the mental health of visitors who choose to engage with disturbing or tragic content.

   Visitation That's Cause for Controversy: Should Certain Sites Remain Closed?

   The topic of whether or not particular locations should continue to be off-limits to the general public is sure to be a contentious one. This highlights the moral conundrums that are inherent with dark tourism.

6. **Protecting Sites and Their Surroundings in the Interest of Environmental Conservation and Sustainability**

   Tourism Methods That Are Friendly To The Environment

   Fostering practices that contribute to the long-term profitability of these places is essential to achieving sustainability in the dark tourism industry. This involves reducing the impact that the high volume of visitor traffic has on the ecosystem and taking other steps toward conservation.

   Preservation of Cultural Resources and Advocacy for These

   It is essential to the continued economic vitality of these places that advocates for the preservation of historical and cultural sites. The continuous acknowledgment and protection of these locations can be ensured through partnerships with groups that are dedicated to preserving history and with governmental agencies.

   Community Development Efforts and Programs

   Key to the practice of sustainable site management is the implementation of community development activities that are to the advantage of the local residents. These initiatives may include educational programs, job creation efforts, and efforts to preserve the community's cultural traditions, all of which add to the community's overall well-being.

7. **Obstacles and the Prospects for the Future of Dark Tourism: A Winding Road Ahead**

The constant development of new technologies, the introduction of exciting new travel places, and the persistence of difficult moral questions will shape the future of dark tourism. It is a field that recognizes the need for sensitivity and respect while also attempting to strike a balance between the pursuit of knowledge and the need to remember.

The future of dark tourism promises to be an adventure filled with technical advancements, educational initiatives, emerging places, and ethical conundrums. Those that are active in this business will need to negotiate a complex route in order to achieve their goals of preserving the authenticity of history while also developing a greater comprehension of times gone by. As we speculate about what the future holds for dark tourism, we are reminded of the continuing ability of these locations to instruct, commemorate, and form the collective memory of our society.

9.1 Trends and predictions for the future of morbid attractions

Morbid attractions, which are a subset of dark tourism, continue to captivate a wide variety of people who are interested in exploring the spooky, the macabre, and the unknown. The future of these attractions will be shaped by the changing preferences of visitors, the progression of technology, the examination of ethical issues, and the emergence of new locations. In this in-depth investigation, we dig into the trends and predictions that will shape the landscape of morbid attractions in the coming years, from the incorporation of cutting-edge technology to the development of new sites and the difficult balance between curiosity and respect. This ranges from the incorporation of cutting-edge technology to the emergence of new sites and includes the delicate balance between curiosity and respect.

1. **An Overview of the Mysteries Behind Haunted Attractions and Their Continuing Development**
   The popularity of macabre tourist destinations, such as haunted houses and ghost tours, as well as immersion experiences in the occult, has increased over the past several years. The landscape of these sites is undergoing substantial changes as a direct result of the growing interest among tourists in investigating the more sinister parts of human history and the supernatural. This investigation takes us on a tour through the trends and predictions that will influence the future of morbid attractions. Along the way, it provides insights into the diverse world of this fascinating type of entertainment and education.
2. **The Preferences of Visitors and the Demographics of the Audience: Changing Curiosities**
   The shifting tastes of tourists and the shifting demographics of those who seek out these kinds of experiences will have an impact on the development of macabre tourist destinations in the future.
   Generation Z and the Millennials
   The younger generations have demonstrated a significant interest in macabre tourist destinations. They look for one-of-a-kind and all-encompassing experiences that offer a blend of entertainment, learning, and a touch of the macabre.

Trends in Health Care and Personal Care
Some tourists seek out macabre tourist destinations as a type of "dark tourism therapy." They utilize these encounters as a means to confront their anxieties, work through their feelings, and interact with the most negative aspects of human existence in a setting that is both managed and secure.

Attempts to Avoid Reality While Seeking Thrills
Some tourists go to macabre sites in order to satisfy their need for excitement and their desire to escape reality. They are looking for excitement and adventure, and they believe that having run-ins with the macabre and the supernatural will provide it for them.

3. **The Contribution of Immersive Technology to the Improvement of the Experience of Visitors**

   Both Virtual Reality and Augmented Reality are Available.
   The use of technology such as virtual reality (VR) and augmented reality (AR) can create immersive storytelling experiences, transfer people to strange places, and enhance supernatural encounters.

   Elements That Are Interactive
   Interactive components are increasingly being integrated into macabre attractions. These components provide guests the opportunity to shape the storyline or uncover secrets, resulting in an experience that is both more customized and more interesting.

   Storytelling in a digital format
   The pre- and post-visit experience is increasingly influenced by digital mediums such as websites, smartphone apps, and social media platforms.
   The narrative of the attraction can be interacted with by visitors, who can also access additional content and share their experiences over the internet.

4. **Emerging Locations and Topics: Increasing the Scope of Gruesome Attractions in the World**

   Themes Revolving Around the Supernatural and the Paranormal
   It is anticipated that visitors would continue to have a strong interest in activities and attractions that revolve around the supernatural, such as haunted houses, ghost tours, and psychic readings. People come because they are intrigued by the possibility of making contact with those on the other side or discovering the secrets of the unknown.

   True crimes and ominous events in history
   There has been a recent uptick in the number of grisly tourist destinations that focus on actual crimes, iconic historical events, and unresolved mysteries. These tourist destinations provide guests with a view into some of the more disturbing periods in human history.

   The World of Pop Culture and Its Fans
   The themes that are used in morbid attractions will continue to be influenced

by popular culture, which includes movies, television shows, and literature. The goal for many visitors is to feel as though they have stepped into the shoes of their favorite fictitious or real-life characters.

5. **Ethical Considerations: Finding a Balance Between Curiosity and Respect for Others**

   Honor for the Dead and Compassion for the Victims

   The key ethical difficulty is to find a happy medium between showing respect for those who have passed away and for those who have been affected by tragic occurrences, on the one hand, and the entertainment value of morbid attractions, on the other. The operators of attractions have a responsibility to make an effort to honor the memory of individuals who were involved while also providing meaningful experiences.

   Trying to Stay Away from Exploitation and Sensationalism

   It is essential to strike a balance between the need to entertain people and the importance of showing respect for the material being discussed. The operators of the attractions are responsible for ensuring that they do not exploit or sensationalize any tragedies.

   Participation in the Community and Working Together

   It is necessary to work in collaboration with the local community, relevant stakeholders, and cultural specialists. Operators of macabre attractions ought to make it a priority to check that their wares are compatible with the standards and requirements of the community.

6. **Environmental Impact and Long-Term Sustainability: Safeguarding Existing Locations and Their Surroundings**

   Tourism Methods That Are Friendly To The Environment

   The promotion of measures that contribute to the destinations' continued sustainability over the long term is an essential component of sustainable morbid attractions. This involves reducing the impact that the high volume of visitor traffic has on the ecosystem and taking other steps toward conservation.

   Preservation of Cultural Resources and Advocacy for These

   It is essential to the continued economic vitality of these places that advocates for the preservation of historical and cultural sites. Through continuing collaboration with organizations dedicated to the preservation of heritage and governmental entities, these locations will continue to be recognized and protected.

   Community Development Efforts and Programs

   Key to the practice of sustainable site management is the implementation of community

   development activities that are to the advantage of the local residents. These initiatives may include educational programs, job creation efforts, and efforts to preserve the community's cultural traditions, all of which add to the community's overall well-being.

7. **Expanding Markets, Contributing to Economic and Industrial Growth**
   Influence on the Economy
   The local economy benefits from morbid attractions in a number of ways, including the creation of jobs, the stimulation of the hospitality and entertainment sectors, and the generation of cash from tourism.
   Diversification of Industries
   The sector is growing more diversified, with a greater range of products, which range from tiny experiences catered to a specific niche to major attractions catering to the general public. This variety accommodates a wide range of preferences held by guests.
   Expansion Across the World
   The number of sites that offer macabre tourist attractions is growing all around the world, and this trend can be seen in a variety of nations. As a result of the industry's global expansion, possibilities for cultural interchange and discovery are becoming increasingly available.
8. **The Challenges of the Future: Striking a Balance Between Entertainment and Responsibility**

Striking a Balance Between Entertainment and Learning
It is essential to find a happy medium between delivering pleasure and imparting useful information to the audience. Without making profit out of tragedy, the industry needs to make sure it can continue to serve both of these functions.

Respect for Different Cultures
It is necessary to have a good understanding of and respect for the cultural sensitivities of tourists who come from a variety of backgrounds. It is essential for morbid attractions to cultivate environments that are welcoming and open to all.

Ethical Conundrums and the Obligations of Responsible Management
The sector needs to address ethical challenges and come up with solutions that put responsibility first. This includes deciding which locations are appropriate for the development of attractions and figuring out how to approach potentially delicate subject matter.

The future of macabre attractions will be characterized by a growing market, advances in technology, new locations, and an increasing emphasis on education and responsibility. While the industry figures out how to manage these trends, it will continue to captivate tourists who are interested in exploring the macabre, the spooky, and the unknown. The dynamic and ever-changing landscape of macabre attractions is a reflection of the ever-changing nature of human curiosity as well as the perennial allure of the unknown and the uncanny.

9.2 Sustainability and responsible tourism in dark tourism
The industry of "dark tourism," which consists of going to places linked with death, tragedy, and the macabre, is confronted with a one-of-a-kind set of difficulties and

opportunities in connection with sustainable and responsible tourism. As the industry continues to expand, there is a growing need to find a middle ground that allows for the protection of the historical significance of the locations in question, the provision of educational opportunities, and the negotiation of difficult ethical issues.

In this in-depth investigation, we delve into the multifaceted world of sustainability and responsible tourism in dark tourism, shedding light on the challenges, strategies, and ethical dilemmas that shape the approach that the industry takes to preserving the past while simultaneously fostering meaningful and respectful visitor experiences.

1. **An Introduction Regarding the Importance of Responsible and Sustainable Tourism in the Dark Tourism Industry**
   Sites of "dark tourism" have important historical and cultural significance, and they frequently act as moving reminders of some of humanity's most trying times. It is crucial that these sites have effective administration and curation in order to guarantee that the tales they contain are conserved, honored, and transmitted to visitors in a manner that is both educative and courteous. This method addresses the need to strike a balance between preservation efforts, educational pursuits, and ethical considerations by incorporating sustainability and responsible tourism practices with dark tourism.
   The purpose of this investigation is to provide light on the difficulties and opportunities that come with practicing sustainable and responsible tourism in dark tourism. Site managers and curators contribute to the continuous remembering and understanding of humanity's darkest periods by maintaining the site's historical integrity, delivering valuable educational experiences, and managing tough ethical problems. Their unwavering commitment to the cause of historical preservation guarantees that the tales associated with these locations will continue to fascinate and influence future generations.
2. **Preserving and ensuring the historical integrity of the site while preserving its authenticity**
   Strategies for Conserving Resources
   The implementation of efficient conservation measures helps to ensure that the physical structures and artifacts found at these sites are preserved in their original state. For the purpose of ensuring that the historical artifacts and relics retain their original authenticity, conservationists implement practices such as repair, upkeep, and documentation.
   Reduction of Human and Other Impacts on the Environment
   Some of the more sinister tourist destinations are found in ecologically fragile areas, which call for vigilant environmental control. Site managers must give primary focus to striking a healthy balance between the effects of visitor traffic and the maintenance of natural surroundings.
   Planning for the Long Term Conservation of Resources

The planning for the long-term preservation of these sites requires anticipating potential difficulties in the future and putting preventative safeguards into place to protect the historical authenticity of the locations. This typically involves the creation of detailed maintenance schedules as well as the application of environmentally friendly procedures.

3. **Communicating the Past and Its Significance Through Educational Experiences**

    Exhibits and Displays That Offer an Interpretive Perspective

    The process of curation frequently entails the creation of interpretive exhibitions and displays that offer historical context and make it easier for visitors to comprehend the material. To make the educational experience more engaging for visitors, these exhibitions could incorporate artifacts, multimedia presentations, or interactive components.

    Educational Programs and Tours Guided by Professionals

    Visitors can gain a better understanding of the historical significance of these locations through
    the implementation of educational programs and the organization of guided tours. The provision of in-depth information and the cultivation of meaningful involvement are both significantly aided by the presence of knowledgeable guides and instructors.

    Platforms for Digital and Virtual Education and Instruction

    The use of digital and virtual learning platforms has become a regular practice in the curation of dark tourist sites as a direct result of the advancements that have been made in technology in recent years. Both on-site and remote visitors can take part in instructional activities that are easily navigable and immersive thanks to these platforms.

4. **The Experience of Visitors and Their Participation: Striking a Balance Between Sensitivity and Impact**

    Support and Well-Being on an Emotional Level

    The administrators of these sites typically provide emotional support tools and information to visitors in order to assist them in navigating their experiences in a manner that is both healthy and courteous. This is because the managers are aware of the possible emotional impact that visiting these sites may have.

    Interaction with Visitors and Participation from Audiences

    It is of the utmost importance to promote visitor participation with and engagement with the historical material. Visitors are able to obtain a more in-depth understanding of the significance of these locations when chances for reflection, conversation, and personal connection are made available to them.

    Ability to Participate and Accessibility

    It is vital, in order to accommodate a wide variety of visitors, to make tourist destinations as accessible and welcoming as possible. This may entail making accommodations for those who have impairments, providing literature in multiple languages, and cultivating an atmosphere that is sensitive to and respectful of different cultural traditions.

5. **Navigating Sensitive Narratives While Considering Ethical Considerations**
   Honor and Dignity Owed to the Dead and the Living
   It is of the utmost importance to ensure that both the emotional well-being of survivors and the dignity of the departed be respected. Storytelling is an important part of any site, and site managers and curators have a responsibility to approach it with empathy and cultural sensitivity in order to ensure that the narratives offered are factual and respectful.

   Finding a Middle Ground Between Education and Sensationalism
   It is essential to achieve a healthy equilibrium between the provision of educational opportunities and the avoidance of sensationalism. In the process of curation, historical authenticity and a comprehensive understanding should take precedence over any sort of exploitation or reduction of the significance of the events in question.

   Participation in the Community and Working Together
   It is necessary to engage with local communities and stakeholders to ensure that the administration and curation of dark tourist sites are aligned with the values and requirements of the community in order to guarantee that dark tourist sites are safe for visitors. Collaborative efforts encourage mutual respect and understanding, which contributes to an approach that is more thorough and ethical to the management of the site.

6. **Adopting Sustainable Practices in Order to Ensure Viability in the Long Term**
   Fostering behaviors that promote the long-term viability of these destinations from both a cultural and environmental point of view is an essential component of sustainable tourism when it comes to the management and curation of dark tourist sites.

   Community Development Efforts and Programs
   Key to the practice of sustainable site management is the implementation of community development activities that are to the advantage of the local residents. These initiatives may include educational programs, job creation efforts, and efforts to preserve the community's cultural traditions, all of which add to the community's overall well-being.

   Efforts Made Towards the Conservation of the Environment
   It is absolutely necessary to use environmentally friendly methods in order to protect the natural environment that surrounds these places. The ecological integrity of the region can be protected through the implementation of conservation measures and the reduction of the ecological impact that visitor traffic has on the area.

Preservation of Cultural Resources and Advocacy for These

It is essential to the continued economic vitality of these places that advocates for the preservation of historical and cultural sites. It is common practice for managers and curators of these sites to work together with historical preservation groups and governmental entities in order to ensure that these places continue to get attention and protection.

7. **Creativity and Flexibility in the Face of Rapid Change Evolving with the Times**

Combining of Various Technologies

The incorporation of technology into the process of museum curation, such as providing visitors with virtual reality experiences, interactive exhibitions, and digital archives, not only improves the overall experience for the visitors but also encourages a more in-depth comprehension of the historical events being presented.

Instruction on Sensitivity to Culture

It is absolutely necessary to provide employees and guides with cultural sensitivity training in order to make sure that interactions with visitors are polite and welcoming to all people. When you have an understanding of a variety of viewpoints and historical circumstances, you may present stories in a way that is more nuanced and sympathetic to the audience.

The Ability to Readjust to Altering Narratives

The ongoing process of historical inquiry and discovery causes historical narratives to vary, and as a result, site managers and curators are required to adjust their techniques of storytelling to appropriately reflect these changes. For the purpose of giving visitors with a thorough understanding of the events that took place at these places, it is necessary to keep historical information accurate and to ensure that the material is up to date.

Sustainability and responsible tourism in the dark tourism industry come with a heavy burden of responsibility, which includes the duty to preserve the history while also providing visitors with experiences that are meaningful and considerate. Site managers and curators, who are devoted to maintaining the historical integrity of these places, make sure that the tales that the sites hold will continue to be relevant and powerful for future generations. They contribute to the continuous recollection and comprehension of humanity's darkest events, so leaving a legacy of compassion and knowledge that is unaffected by the passage of time by striking a balance between preservation, education, and ethical issues.

9.3 How global events and shifts in society impact the industry

The dynamic and ever-evolving field of "dark tourism," which entails going to places linked with death, sorrow, and the macabre, is a sector that is deeply impacted by both global events and shifts in society norms and values. The essence of this one-of-a-kind type of tourism, as well as its development over time, has been continually molded by historical, political, cultural, and technical shifts. In this extensive investigation, we dig into the varied ways in which global events and cultural trends have impacted the dark tourism business. These impacts range from the development of tourist preferences and the emergence of emergent places to ethical considerations and the use of technology.

1. **A Brief Introduction to the Evolving Landscape of the Dark Tourism Industry**

   The tourism industry that deals in dark attractions is distinguished by the natural connection it has to historical happenings, cultural narratives, and societal viewpoints. The dark tourism sector is not immune to the changes that the world is continuously undergoing in a variety of spheres, as the world itself is always evolving. This investigation tries to discover how global events and movements in society have impacted the business in a variety of ways, including influencing the preferences of visitors, reshaping locations, posing ethical challenges, and providing chances for innovation.

   As we continue on our journey through the intersections of dark tourism with global events and

   societal upheavals, we will get insights into the dynamic and ever-changing landscape of an industry that straddles history, memory, education, and entertainment. As we continue on this journey, we will gain insights into the dynamic and ever-changing landscape of an industry that straddles history, memory, education, and entertainment.

2. **Preferred Activities of Visitors and Their Evolving Curiosities and Interests**

   Historical Accounts and Their Place in Context

   Events that occur on a global scale, such as anniversaries of pivotal historical moments, might reignite interest in the connected tourist destinations known as "dark tourism."

   The goal for visitors is to become involved with the historical setting in order to have a more in-depth comprehension of the occurrences that took place.

   An Awareness of Both Politics and Culture

   Changes in a society's level of political and cultural consciousness can have an effect on the preferences of tourists. It is common for movements that advocate for social justice, human rights, and historical acknowledgment to lead to a rise in interest in dark tourism places associated with the topics being advocated for.

   New Ideas and Concepts

   Emerging themes and topics of interest in global society, such as the preservation of the natural environment or the management of public health concerns, might contribute to the creation of new destinations for dark tourism. These places are popular tourist destinations because they cater to the modern preoccupations and interests of its guests.

3. **Newly Emerging Destinations: Historic and Culturally Significant Places**
   Newly Discovered Historical Landmarks
   In the wake of global events, hitherto obscure historical locations are frequently thrust into the spotlight. New study and findings may lead to the discovery of locations with historical value, which will increase the appeal of these locations to those who are interested in dark tourism.
   Places of Historical and Contemporary Political and Cultural Significance
   Sites that become culturally or politically significant owing to global events, such as landmark anniversaries or shifting political climates, may draw people looking to interact with the modern resonance of these locations. Examples of such global events include changing political climates and landmark anniversaries.
   Current Trends in the Tourism Industry
   Destinations for contemporary forms of dark tourism are emerging as a direct result of recent
   occurrences such as pandemics, terrorist acts, and natural disasters. People go to these locations in order to feel more connected to recent history and to better engage with the feelings and effects that these events have.
4. **Moral Considerations: Struggling to Find a Balance Between Sensitivity and Respect**
   Respect and Dignity for the Person Who Has Passed Away
   Events on a global scale frequently spark greater conversations on the dignity and respect that should be accorded to the departed, particularly in the context of widespread natural disasters or historical atrocities. The sector needs to address these topics with the utmost caution and cultural awareness in order to be successful.
   Trying to Stay Away from Exploitation and Sensationalism
   As a result of the rapid dissemination of news and information in today's globe, the tourist industry must exercise extreme caution to prevent the portrayal of dark tourism destinations as exploitative or sensationalist. The industry as a whole needs to maintain a responsible approach to storytelling in order to prevent sensationalized accounts from diminishing the significance of the events.
   Participation in the Community and Working Together
   Changes in the viewpoints and norms of a society can have an effect on the way dark tourist destinations are managed and maintained. It is absolutely necessary to work together with the local communities and the many stakeholders to ensure that the management of the site is in line with the expectations and values of the community. This engagement contributes to increased levels of mutual regard and comprehension.
5. **The Integration of New Technologies to Improve the Experience of Site Visitors**
   Both Virtual Reality and Augmented Reality are Available.

The experience that tourists enjoy at dark tourism locations has been completely transformed as a result of developments in technology such as virtual reality (VR) and augmented reality (AR). These technologies provide interactive and immersive storytelling, which takes visitors into the past and gives them the opportunity to interact with historical content.

Mobile applications and interactive displays are available.
The use of interactive exhibitions, mobile applications, and digital platforms has evolved into a typical strategy for improving the experience of visitors. The educational and entertaining value of these platforms is enhanced since users have access to additional content, interactive components, and the possibility for self-guided exploration.

Multimedia and the Use of Digital Narratives
A more in-depth connection with historical narratives can be achieved through the use of digital storytelling techniques such as multimedia presentations, documentaries, and online platforms. The sector makes extensive use of digital resources in order to disseminate instructional material and attract a larger audience.

6. **Contemporary Dark Tourism in the Context of Global Crises: Maneuvering Through Sensitive Narratives**
The dark tourism business is faced with a number of one-of-a-kind obstacles and opportunities as a result of contemporary world crises such as natural catastrophes, pandemics, and acts of terrorism.

The Resilience and Recovery of Humans
Visitors are frequently drawn to locations linked with modern crises in order to experience the human capacity for resilience and recovery. These visits provide a one-of-a-kind opportunity to engage with stories of people who have overcome adversity and found peace.

Consideration and deference are required.
The industry must walk a tight line between offering educational experiences and understanding the emotional impact that these events have on people in order to be successful. Those visitors who have been through a difficult time in their own lives may find comfort and understanding via their trips here.

The Importance of History in Understanding Current Occurrences
The passage of time transforms events that were formerly considered contemporary into historical events. The industry needs to take a cautious approach to these narratives, putting an emphasis on the significance of their contributions and the lasting effect they have on society.

7. **Responding to Emergencies and Managing Risks While Maintaining an Attitude of Respect**

Communication and Relations with the Public

It is essential to maintain strong lines of communication with attendees and the general public both during and after major events. The provision of information, updates, and resources to tourists as part of crisis management is essential in order to keep them abreast of any possible shifts in their itineraries.

Respect for the Communities That Have Been Affected

The business sector is obligated to display respect and compassion toward the communities and individuals who have survived catastrophes. In order to effectively handle a crisis, it is necessary to engage with the affected populations in a way that is both responsible and empathetic.

Adaptive Methods and Techniques

In order to effectively respond to a crisis, one frequently needs to be flexible in regard to shifting conditions, shifting visitor expectations, and shifting safety concerns. The sector must put into place adaptable solutions in order to continue providing meaningful experiences for visitors while simultaneously honoring the significance of the events.

At the intersection of history, memory, educational pursuits, and entertaining activities is where you'll find the dark tourism business. The sector is undergoing significant change in tandem with the ongoing process of world shaping that is being driven by global events and societal transformations. The dynamic and ever-evolving nature of this one-of-a-kind style of tourism is highlighted by the interaction that exists between dark tourism, society, and world events. The dark tourism sector continues to deliver meaningful experiences for individuals who are interested in engaging with the darker sides of human history and society by remaining sensitive to the interests of visitors, maintaining historical narratives in a conscientious manner, and capitalizing on improvements in technological innovation.

www.ingramcontent.com/pod-product-compliance
Lightning Source LLC
LaVergne TN
LVHW010218070526
838199LV00062B/4645